The Day I Shot
a Squirrel

John Francis Smith III as a boy (*family photo*)

The Day I Shot a Squirrel

STORIES OF A TWENTIETH CENTURY AMERICAN BOYHOOD

John Francis Smith III

VILLANOVA, PENNSYLVANIA

2022

To my parents, Jay and Mary Smith,
and to Deedee, David, and Linda,
my first companions on the journey

Contents

Preface   xi
Community   xiii

I. Setting the Stage   3

The Mighty Hudson River   3
Creation of the Village of Irvington   6
The Great Irvington-Tarrytown Post Office War   6
Twentieth Century Irvington   8
A Walk Down Main Street   10

II. The Smiths Come to Irvington   14

Genealogy 101   14
Putting Down Roots in Irvington   20
I Arrive on the Scene   22

III. The War Years   24

Diversion to Hampton Roads, Virginia   25
The Traumatic Birth of My Sister Deedee   26
Dad Ships Out to China   27

The War Ended, We Return to West Clinton Avenue   28
My Grandmother's Place on Dows Lane   29

IV. Postwar Period   31

My First Career Plan   31
My Fascination with Traffic on the Hudson River   33
Old Gray Warriors on Their Way to Retirement   33
Progress: Television and Beyond   36
The Today Show: "Hey, I Know Him!"   40

V. Family Life   41

My Family Grows   41
The Beatles Take America by Storm   43
Cream Rises to the Top   44
Leadership Training at the Yellow Brick Pile   45
Sledding on West Clinton   47
The Joy of Christmas—and of Waiting for It   50
Of Cats, Vises, and Birthdays   55

VI. School Days   58

Pennybridge—Old Name, Old School   58
Riding on the Aqueduct   59
Stern Mrs. Bishop   62
Chalk Flies in Math Class   63
Life on the Playground   64
Channeling Benny Goodman   66

VII. The World Beyond Irvington   70

Saturday Was a Workday   70
The Trip to Coney Island That Wasn't   75

Family Vacations   77
The Catfish   79
Sailing at Gilbert Lake State Park   82
Capturing the Wild Red Eft   85
Arrowheads from the Stone Age   87
Searching for the "Inverted Jenny"   90

VIII. Lessons   94

I Try Smoking   94
Sports Medicine: "Just Rub It Off"   95
The Day I Shot a Squirrel   98

Epilogue   106
Acknowledgments   107

Preface

This book is a collection of stories about what I did and what happened to me when I was kid growing up in the 1940s and early 1950s.

A lot of momentous things were taking place in the larger world during that era. World War II shook our country and the entire globe in the first half of the 1940s. After the war, the millions of men and women who had been serving in our armed forces came home and resumed civilian life. Together, they transformed American living patterns, with many of them building new lives in what came to be called the "suburbs." Bolstered by pent-up demand, the U.S. economy enjoyed a postwar boom. Peace was short-lived, though. A new war, a "Cold War" between the United States and the Soviet Union, emerged to take the place of the one just finished. Another armed conflict broke out on the Korean peninsula in the 1950s. Meanwhile, not far behind the scenes, racial injustice issues festered here in the United States. These would boil over in the 1960s and occupy my attention in the years ahead.

Some of those large-scale events affected my growing-up years. But even as they swirled about, my parents were determined that I should have, to the best of their ability, a normal childhood. In this, they were largely successful. My life unfolded on its own terms, enabling me to live the boyhood described in these stories.

Much has happened since then. Inventions have changed the way people live. Customs have changed. The pace of daily living has accelerated. In light of all of that, it isn't surprising that the lives of those of us who grew up in the middle of the past century will be seen as different from the lives of children today. The stories in this book are unique to me and my era as a result. At the same time, they contain a degree of universality. They are quintessentially American stories, and their themes transcend the age and specific settings in which they took place. I hope, therefore, that you will not only enjoy the stories for their own sake but also discover echoes of your own experiences resonating within them.

Community

Except for a few years during World War II, I grew up in a village called Irvington—sometimes Irvington-on-Hudson—in the state of New York. It is a small community, located twenty miles north of a very big community, the city of New York. As the name suggests, the village is right next to the Hudson River.

The village had only a few thousand residents. There was an intimacy to it. The old cliché about small towns was true: Virtually everyone there knew virtually everyone else there. It was a safe place to knock around in. This feeling started with my parents, who loved me and provided everything they could for me. But it went beyond that, too. Wherever I went in Irvington, I was surrounded by a nurturing community.

As I grew older, I went farther afield and felt secure in doing so. Good roots had promoted strong wings. Together, they gave me a sense of self-confidence and adventure, characteristics that have helped me throughout my life.

The Day I Shot
a Squirrel

CHAPTER 1

Setting the Stage

The Mighty Hudson River

Irvington didn't just happen. It was the product of many forces. Not the least of these was the Hudson River, the mighty body of water that flows past the village and gave it its life from the beginning.

The Hudson rises in northern New York State. Its headwaters are wild and beautiful, justly celebrated over the years by both artists and writers. A whole school of painting—the famous Hudson River School—was devoted to capturing that beauty. (The luxuriant autumnal scene on the front cover of this book was painted by Jervis McEntee, one of its members.)

From its mountainous origins, the Hudson flows south for several hundreds of miles, past upstate farms and communities, soon reaching the state capital in Albany. The historically important Erie Canal connects with the Hudson at Troy, from which point the canal heads west toward the Great Lakes. The river, however, continues its southerly course, picking up additional mass from streams on both sides. It continues down past the Catskill Mountains on its western side and Franklin D. Roosevelt's old home at

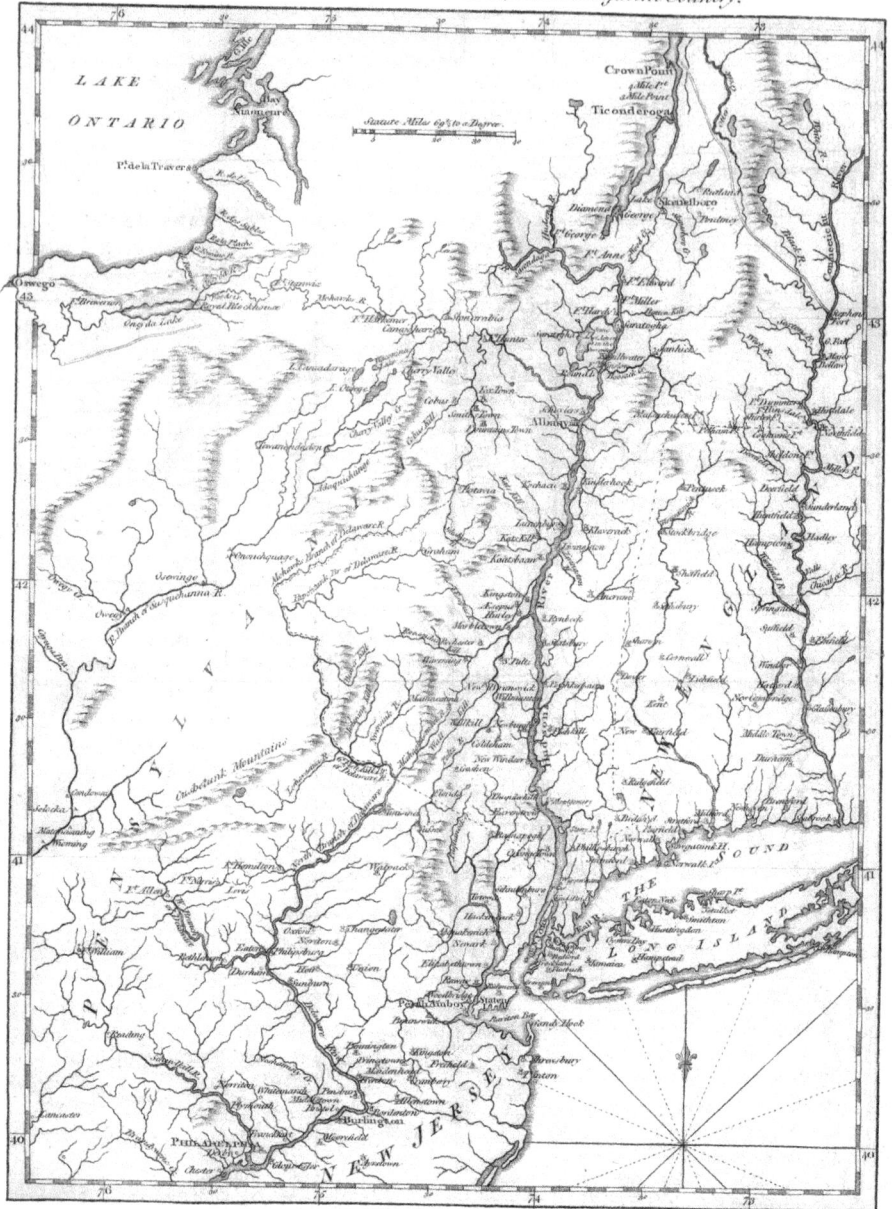

This map of the Hudson River was published in the London-based *Gentleman's Magazine* in 1778 during the Revolutionary War; Irvington had not yet been founded (*private collection of JFSIII*)

Hyde Park on its eastern side. Several miles farther down, it arrives at West Point, the site of Revolutionary War activity and now the home of the U.S. Military Academy. From there it continues downstream, spilling into a wider portion of the river, the vast sea-like expanse just above Irvington that the Dutch called the "Tappan Zee." By this time, it contains a massive amount of water. The effect is striking. The river has the look of a boa constrictor that has recently swallowed a large animal and has a bulge midway along its length. After the Tappan Zee, the river course slims again, forcing the water to move more rapidly. The Hudson reaches Irvington's waterfront in this quickened state. In the remaining miles, it flows past the Palisades, past New York City's Manhattan Island, and past the Statue of Liberty, finally arriving at New York Harbor.

The Wecquaesgeek Indians, a branch of the Lenape or Delaware Indians, were the first human beings to navigate the river and the first to live on the riverside land that would become Irvington. Centuries later, the Europeans arrived. In 1524, Giovanni da Verrazzano, a Florentine explorer, sailed into what is now New York Harbor and declared that he had "discovered" the river. No doubt, the Indians begged to differ. On September 3, 1609, Henry Hudson, then in the service of the Dutch East India Company, and his crew sailed into the river and continued upstream to what is now Albany. It is from this achievement that the river derives its name. Dutch settlers followed. In due course, they were supplanted by English ones. The arrival of the successive waves of European settlers had a devastating effect on the Indians, setting in motion their ultimate displacement.

Slowly, roadways were established, linking the settlements along the river with each other and connecting them to New Amsterdam—later New York—to the south. Many of the early roads followed old Indian trails. In those early years, however, the Hudson continued to provide the most important means of transportation. It was the lifeblood of the communities along its banks. Over the centuries that followed, the wide and navigable Hudson would become one of the most commercially important rivers in the nation and would figure in some of the most important moments in American history.

Creation of the Village of Irvington

By the early nineteenth century, two communities, Dearman and Abbotsford, had developed alongside the river in the vicinity of current-day Irvington. Dearman, the bigger of the two, had some six hundred citizens and a hotel. The Hudson River Railroad had arrived and with it a small ferry that would take you across the Hudson to Piermont, a community on the western side. Abbotsford was smaller. It had developed below what is now East and West Clinton Avenue, a street that would later figure in my story.

At the time, the prominent early American author Washington Irving was living on the northern edge of Dearman in a home called Sunnyside. Sunnyside was actually in Tarrytown, the community adjacent to Dearman. That circumstance, however, did not deter the citizens of either Dearman or Abbotsford. They voted to combine forces in 1854 and name the combination "Irvington" after the great writer. They did this notwithstanding the potential for upset in nearby Tarrytown. A new village was born!

The Great Irvington-Tarrytown Post Office War

At the risk of getting ahead of the timeline, let's take a brief side trip to find out how Irvington and Tarrytown might get along in the future. We will travel by time machine and touch down in the year 1943.

During that year, the country was in the middle of World

Currier and Ives print of "Sunnyside," the residence of famous author Washington Irving (*New York Public Library, cropped by Beyond My Ken; courtesy of Wikimedia Commons*)

War II. All Americans, as one, were engaged in helping to prosecute the war. One might have expected, therefore, that the upstanding towns of Irvington and Tarrytown, both of them replete with fine citizens, would be pulling together, that they would act together in all matters in mutual support of the war effort and each other.

Instead, the two towns had a war of their own.

The underlying cause of the conflict was a decision by the federal government to honor American writers through the issuance of a series of new postage stamps, the Great American Authors series. Needless to say, Washington Irving, who wrote "The Legend of Sleepy Hollow" and "Rip Van Winkle," was regarded as a Great American Author. To honor him, a stamp bearing his image would be created for the series. All were in agreement, certainly all of the folks in the two towns, that this was an excellent thing to do.

There was just one matter that needed to be resolved: Which town's post office would be favored with the right to issue the stamp on the first day it was to be rolled out to the public?

Post offices and their loyal townsfolk do not take such matters lightly. To be the site of the first issuance—to have a "First Day of Issue" envelope designed to bear the stamp and have the stamp and envelope canceled right there in your own post office—was a signal honor and privilege. One worth fighting for. And so, they did. Irvington claimed the right because, after all, it was named Irvington by vote of the good people who merged the Dearman and Abbotsford communities in 1854. On the other hand, Tarrytown claimed the right because, after all, Sunnyside was in Tarrytown. Irving may have been dead for nearly ninety years, but for goodness' sake, doesn't having his old residence in your town count for something?

The battle raged. There could be only one victor in this conflict. It's true that, at the age of two, I had no personal involvement in the conflagration. And it's also true that I was probably riding a tricycle hundreds of miles away at the time. Still, I have no doubt that every argument that could be made on the side of Irvington was made and that every string that could be pulled was pulled. Nor do I doubt that, if I had been of age, I would have joined the fray lustily on Irvington's behalf. Sadly, however, the decision of the U.S. Postal Service went the wrong way. Irvington was not chosen. The dark forces of Tarrytown had prevailed. On a fateful day in 1943, the Tarrytown Post Office exercised its right to introduce the new stamp to its eager citizens and, for all who wished one, to postmark it on a "First Day of Issue" envelope.

Twentieth Century Irvington

Irvington was a beautiful community in the 1940s and 1950s. It remains largely that way today. Standing above the river that flows majestically beneath it, the town is well laid out and has plenty of open space. It prides itself on being "clean and green," attractive and quiet.

The village is connected to the communities above and below it by Route 9, the Albany Post Road. This roadway parallels the river, running north and south through the town. Route 9 is better known as "Broadway." Broadway is an extension of New York City's "Great White Way," the site of over-the-top celebrations of New Year's Eve. One can start in New York City and follow Broadway north right up through each of the towns along the river, all the way up to Albany.

Down closer to the river and paralleling it is a railway, now part of Metro North, which was once the Hudson Division of the New York Central Railroad. The railroad was important because it provided quick transportation into New York City. My father used it to commute to his job in the Financial District.

But it was also, in legal parlance, "an attractive nuisance," something that could lure kids in and do them harm. I had

View of a passenger train and the Hudson River beyond (*iStock, with permission*)

a set of model trains in my basement, but I loved the real ones, particularly the very long freight trains. I frequently went down to watch them, counting the cars as they rolled by. It was a potentially dangerous pastime, and my friends and I made it even more so. There was an electrified "third rail" that provided power to the trains that used the line. To touch it was to court death. Every now and then an unfortunate dog would try to squeeze under the third rail and get electrocuted. Nevertheless, we would sneak down and lay pennies and dimes on the tracks so we could watch them get squashed by oncoming trains. They made cool souvenirs. This activity was against every rule in the book. Fortunately, we never got caught—or electrocuted!

The village's main street ran east-west, sloping down from Broadway to the train tracks and river on its lower end. This street was the center of village life, and we will therefore turn to it next.

A Walk Down Main Street

There were lots of reasons to visit Main Street. This was where you could find almost everything you needed. In kindergarten, in tenth grade, and for many grades in between, you went to school at the Main Street School. The mayor's office and the police department were on Main Street. The town library was on Main Street. And you could shop there, too.

At the upper end, that is, at the corner of Main and Broadway, there stood a classic, old-fashioned drugstore called—What else?—the Corner Store. In addition to a pharmacy, it had a soda fountain, and it sold magazines. It was a great place to hang out. You could buy a soda and, if you were careful and didn't bother anyone, you could nurse it long enough to read, surreptitiously, all the comic books on the rack in the back of the store. I did this a lot.

View of Main Street, Irvington, from the Hudson River (*photo by Edna Kornberg; courtesy of the Irvington Historical Society*)

Several doors down was the office of Dr. Chesley Smith. He was our family physician. My mother marched me in to see Dr. Smith whenever my ears, nose, or throat needed checking, or it was time for a shot. Farther down Main Street, more or less clustered together, were the town hall, the police and fire departments, the town library, and the first school I ever attended.

I remember the Irvington Town Hall very well. In addition to the offices of the municipality, it contained the town library and an auditorium with a small stage where productions were held from time to time. Once a year the schoolchildren of the village were invited to perform on the stage.

This event was developed as a gift to the community by one of its then most famous residents, Ted Mack. Few will remember Ted Mack today, but in the forties and fifties he was a prominent TV host on a nationally broadcast television show called *Ted Mack and the Original Amateur Hour.* Acts from all over the country were featured on his program and many of the performers would go on to professional careers. You might say that it was a mid-twentieth century forerunner of twenty-first century hits like *American Idol* and *America's Got Talent.* The children of Irvington were not at the level of those chosen to perform on TV! Nevertheless, each year Mack unpacked his genial sense of humor, came to the town hall, and presided over a couple of hours of local entertainment. As a budding young clarinetist at the time, I had formed a German oom-pah band. We went on stage and played a Bavarian number of some sort. My sister Deedee and two little friends, looking adorable in yellow slickers, sang "Once There Were Three Fishermen." Squeaky violins were played, and memorized poems were recited. Virtually any kid who wanted to be on stage was given the chance. Mack would announce you, and you would do your act. The audience of parents and friends loved it all.

On the opposite side of the street were other establishments of note. One was Lenny's Barber Shop. I liked Lenny. Every three weeks or so he cut my hair. He was a friendly guy, and his shop always had some older men sitting around talking "guy stuff." In the late forties, which wasn't long after the end of World War II, he had piles of tabloids to read. They were filled with sensational stuff about the aftermath of the war. A typical story might declare something like, "Hitler did not commit suicide as the Allies closed in on Berlin but is instead hiding out in South America." This was heady stuff for a kid to read. Lenny was community minded. Each Halloween, like many of his fellow merchants, he would let us paint his shop window with ghoulish creations. For this one holiday, Main Street was transformed into a parade of ghosts, goblins, witches, and leering cats.

Farther down the street you found Mr. Wistrand's tailor shop. Mr. Wistrand took care of our dress-up clothes when they needed cleaning, pressing, or mending. He was a kindly gentleman with a white moustache and a twinkle in his eye. He spoke with a Swiss accent that intrigued me. I guess that he did a good job on the clothes, but he was an inveterate cigar smoker. Everything we entrusted to his care came back smelling like one of his cigars.

Across the street was a small outlet of the grocery chain called Gristede's. With no supermarkets nearby, my mother often did food shopping there. It was an interesting place. You could stand at the counter and, after you placed your order, a clerk would reach up with a long pole with a gripper on the end and snag each item off the shelf for you.

That was fine, but I liked Becker's better. Becker's was a 5-&-10-cent store located near Gristede's. It sold small toys and candy. Whenever I happened to be along with my mother at Gristede's, I would excuse myself for a quick inspection of the merchandise at Becker's. This was dangerous, particularly after I started getting an allowance. The temptation was great and sometimes irresistible. My sweet tooth was in control. If I had any loose coins with me, they would quickly burn a hole in my pocket. I'd pick up some Lifesavers or a handful of Tootsie Rolls or whatever else I craved at the moment, fetch out a nickel or a dime, plunk it on the counter, and start consuming the candy on the spot. Oh my, did it taste good!

At the bottom of the street there were some industries, some corporate offices, a movie studio, and Matthiessen Park, a small riverside park.

CHAPTER II

The Smiths Come to Irvington

Genealogy 101

My father and my mother came from different parts of the country and had different backgrounds, but in some ways their personal histories were similar.

My Father's Side

My father, John Francis Smith Jr., was born in 1913 and grew up in Frederick, Maryland. He was the son of John Francis Smith and Emily Nelson Maulsby.

The original John Francis Smith, my father's father and thus my grandfather, was a prominent lawyer in Frederick. He traced his roots to Lord Baltimore, the founder of the Colony of Maryland. Maryland was settled largely by Roman Catholics, many of whom left England, beginning in 1634, in order to practice their Catholic faith freely in the New World. Accordingly, my grandfather was Catholic.

Emily Nelson Maulsby, my grandmother, traced her roots to a series of lawyers and state representatives in the Maulsby clan. Among them was her grandfather (and therefore my great-great-grandfather) Colonel William Pinckney

My paternal grandparents, the original John Francis Smith and Emily Nelson Maulsby, with my father, John Francis Smith Jr., as a baby (*family photo*)

Maulsby. Col. Maulsby had a distinguished career in the civic and political life of Maryland. Maryland was a "border state" at the time of the Civil War. Some of its citizens sympathized with the North and some sympathized with the South. When the war broke out, Col. Maulsby sided with the North and recruited fellow Frederick citizens to join the 1st Potomac Home Brigade, which he commanded. His brigade later fought and distinguished itself at the Battle of Gettysburg in July 1863. There is a monument to the brigade on the battlefield, not far from the well-known location of Spanglers Spring.

Unlike the Smiths, the Maulsbys were not Catholics. They were Episcopalians, and thus my grandmother was brought up as an Episcopalian.

Differences in religion are often a problem today, but back then they were a really big deal. When my grandparents married, my Catholic grandfather agreed with my Episcopalian grandmother to allow any children they would have

Left: Portrait of Col. William Pinckney Maulsby (*photo courtesy of David M. Smith*); *right:* Monument at Gettysburg to the 1st Potomac Home Brigade (*family photo*)

John Francis Smith Jr. in
his twenties (*family photo*)

to be brought up in her Episcopal faith. Thus, my father, John Francis Smith Jr., was brought up as an Episcopalian. Remarkably, this agreement caused my grandfather's church briefly to excommunicate him.

My father would be their only child. Tragically, despite having a robust constitution and a promising future, my grandfather contracted typhoid fever on a hunting trip and died in 1916. My father was only three years old at the time. He would be brought up in Frederick by his mother and her sister, Mary Maulsby. The two sisters must have done a great job. My father grew up to be both athletic and bright. (Years later I would try to beat him at tennis, but he had a formidable topspin forehand. When he was at the top of his game, I could never manage to defeat him!) Dad graduated from Princeton University in 1935 and joined Wood Struthers & Winthrop, a small but prominent investment firm in New York City. This was fine. It was a good opportunity. But for several years, it was not a remunerative one. Dad had many "payless paydays" during the Depression of the 1930s.

Sadly, my father, who had lost his father at the age of three, would lose his mother in 1939. That was two years before I was born. As a result, I never knew either my Grandfather Smith or my Grandmother Smith.

My Mother's Side

My mother's family was as deeply rooted in the Hudson River Valley as my father's was in Frederick, Maryland. Her father, John Dows Mairs, was a grandson of David Dows, a major grain dealer in New York City and a wealthy citizen of the Village of Irvington. Her mother, Mary Dake Mattison Mairs, was descended from a long and prosperous line of Mattisons. One of the family's wings can be traced to early settlers of Staten Island, New York, who were Huguenots. The Huguenots had been expelled from France in 1685, when the French king revoked an earlier edict that allowed Protestants to live in Catholic France. They were forced to leave hastily, and their properties were confiscated. They escaped by ship.

Religious discrimination has been a powerful force throughout history. Ancient acts of discrimination—Protestant against Catholic and Catholic against Protestant—caused hundreds of thousands of people to flee their homelands and seek new lives in North America. You will recall that my father's forebears, who were Catholic, felt that they needed to come to the New World because of discrimination against them in England. For my mother's forebears, the discrimination was the other way around. The Huguenots came to America because of discrimination against their Protestant religion in France.

My grandfather, John Dows Mairs, had significant health issues. During his engagement to my grandmother, he came close to death. But my grandmother was determined that he should live. To the amazement of her family, she arranged for them to marry at his hospital bedside and miraculously he recovered. He and my grandmother moved to Hartford, Connecticut, where he took a job in insurance and tried to make a go of it. It did not work out. He and my grandmother then moved to Kinderhook, New York, up along the Hudson River Valley. There they raised squab, a kind of pigeon that was regarded as a delicacy, for upscale restaurants and clubs. This venture, too, was short-lived.

Along the way, they gave birth to two children, my mother and my uncle, Edwin H. Mairs. To us he was Uncle Ned. A few years after my uncle was born, John Dows Mairs died, leaving my grandmother with two children and little in the way of financial resources.

Meanwhile, my grandmother's brother, Joseph Mattison (Uncle Joe to me), had done well. A graduate of Harvard University, he had a successful career in business and moved to a large property in Hastings-on-Hudson, New York, two towns below Irvington. But his life, too, was marred by tragedy. After giving birth to three children, his

Mary Dake Mairs Smith in her twenties (*family photo*)

first wife committed suicide. Uncle Joe was now bereft of a wife, and my grandmother was without means. The logical solution was for my grandmother to move in with him and keep house. This she did, with my mother and Uncle Ned in tow. It may have been logical, but it was a difficult situation, nevertheless.

In the thirties, money was tight. When it came time for college, whatever money my grandmother may have had in the wake of my grandfather's death went to pay for Uncle Ned's education, not my mother's. Though my mother was as bright as he was, he went to Harvard, and she never went beyond secondary school. Such were the sexist choices of the day. Even so, the money spent on Harvard wasn't a good investment. Uncle Ned never graduated. He did go into the Navy and served in World War II, but he never amounted to much after that.

IN SHORT, UP THROUGH the first twenty years of their lives, each of my parents had to endure a degree of hardship. The Great Depression weighed on each of them, as it did on virtually every American. They had each lost a parent. Each had been forced into an alternative living arrangement with another family member while growing up. For each, the path forward was unclear.

Happily, their lives took a turn for the better in the latter half of the 1930s. They had independently joined the Young Adults Group at St. Bartholomew's Church in mid-town Manhattan. There they met and fell in love. Soon afterward, with their mothers—but no fathers—looking on, they married in St. Bartholomew's in 1937.

Putting Down Roots in Irvington

Hoping to raise a family, my parents bought one and a third acres of land in Irvington in 1938. The property was on a semi-rural street called West Clinton Avenue. Like Main Street, West Clinton ran from Broadway down to the river. They hired an architect and, over the next several years, built the house in which my siblings and I would grow up.

I can see the house now in my mind's eye. It was a brick structure and the bricks, initially yellow, were painted white. The architect intended that there be a wing on the south side of the house, and that's what his drawings showed. But my parents put our education before the potential expansion of the house. There would be four of us and big college bills to pay someday. The addition never happened. All around the frieze, just below the cornice, was an elaborate reproduction in wood lathing of the "Greek key" design. This accent had been required by my father. He was a great fan of Greek culture, and particularly of the idea of democracy that the Greeks had developed. He strongly believed in electing public officials democratically. I have often thought of him as an Athenian who was born twenty-four centuries late.

Our home on West Clinton Avenue (*family photo*)

The house was almost perfectly situated. It was in the heart of the Hudson River Valley. My mother's family had a long history in that part of the world. Mom had grown up first in Yonkers and then Hastings-on-Hudson. Her mother, "Grammy" to me, was now living in Irvington in a nearby carriage house. The property was a short, walkable distance from a train station and rail line that served people like my father. Dad could commute to Wood Struthers & Winthrop in Manhattan. The neighborhood was uncrowded but friendly. There was a splendid view of the Hudson from the back porch. And for my siblings and me, when we later showed up, there was a big backyard, with fields and woods beyond. We would explore this bucolic landscape with abandon.

I Arrive on the Scene

My mother brought me into the world on September 24, 1941, at a hospital in nearby White Plains. Of course, I have no recollection of that, nor of my introduction to Irvington a few days later. It's reasonable to surmise, however, that the West Clinton Avenue house was complete enough that my father could bring my mother and my newborn self there, fresh from the hospital.

In the tradition of my grandfather and father, I was baptized John Francis Smith—in my case the name was followed by a Roman numeral III, as the third of the line—at St. Barnabas, the local Episcopal church. Soon afterward, I picked up the name "Franky." Over the years, this gradually became "Johnny" and, after the age of ten, just "John." All these names were bestowed lovingly. If I got into trouble, however, it was "John Francis," as in "John Francis, are you the one who just tracked mud all over the kitchen floor?" A somewhat stern great uncle, the tragic Joseph Mattison, always called me "J.F."

Author enjoying a swim in
a pot, with our English
bull terrier looking on
(family photo)

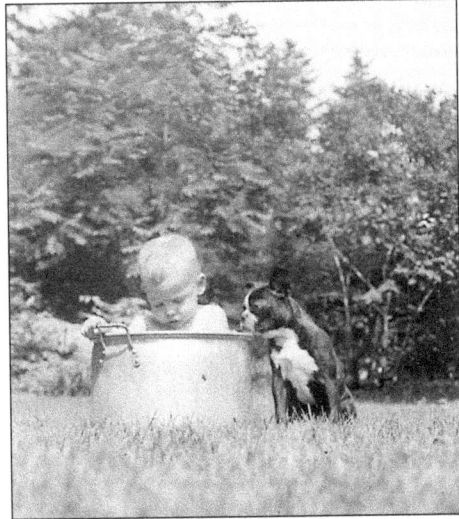

For a few months, we settled into our new lives together. What I know about it comes mostly from family interviews and photo albums. There are pictures of me with our dog, a small English bull terrier, one of my mother's favorite breeds.

In this early period, my mother was making a home for us. My father was developing his routine as a commuter. Grammy, one of my favorite people, was always nearby. A happy family life had begun in Irvington.

However idyllic that existence must have been, it would be short-lived. As a small child, I would learn very little about Irvington. A global war got in the way of that.

CHAPTER III

The War Years

Explosion destroys USS *Shaw* during 1941 attack on Pearl Harbor
(*courtesy of U.S. Navy*)

Diversion to Hampton Roads, Virginia

On December 7, 1941, a Japanese fleet and accompanying airplanes suddenly attacked the U. S. naval base at Pearl Harbor in Honolulu. The United States declared war on Japan shortly afterward. Meanwhile, Nazi Germany had already started a war in Europe, overrunning Belgium and Poland and most of France. Britain was severely threatened. Every night German bombers wreaked destruction on London and England's manufacturing cities. The United States had been lending ships and war supplies to the British, but it was now apparent that that was not enough. Hitler's army seemed invincible. Shortly after the declaration of war on Japan, we declared war on Germany, too.

I was oblivious to all of that at the outset. But my mother and father must have felt the impact of these events and been greatly moved by them. The United States was at war with both Germany and Japan, and a general mobilization of the country had begun. Dad was a proud American citizen and saw it as his duty to enlist. On February 2, 1942, only months after I was born, he joined the U. S. Army. I have no doubt that my mother felt trepidation as a result, but also that she saw it as her duty to support him in his decision.

After a brief stint as a Technician 4th Grade on Governors Island, New York, my father was assigned to the Army's Eastern Signal Corps School at Fort Monmouth, New Jersey. On October 16, 1942, after ninety days of officer training, he received a commission as a First Lieutenant. From there, he was reassigned to active duty as a Signal Supply Officer at the Port of Embarkation at Hampton Roads, Virginia. Dad and Mom rented out the Irvington house. Somehow, they found rental housing near his duty station. My mother and I moved there to be near him.

Hampton Roads was part of a huge military complex that included the naval base at Newport News. The complex involved all the services, the Army, the Navy, and what was then called the Army Air Force, and it was growing bigger by the week. Military preparations dominated the lower end of the Chesapeake Bay. The United States was gearing up to enter the war in a major way. My earliest memories, therefore, are not of Irvington but of Hampton Roads and the huge military facilities nearby. We lived in an apartment as the tenants of Mrs. Paxton. This kindly woman turned out to be not just our landlord but also a great friend and support for my mother. This was fortuitous. My mother was now pregnant with twins.

The Traumatic Birth of My Sister Deedee

On September 15, 1943, my sister Deedee was born. She would later be baptized Mary Dake Smith, the third in a line of Mary Dakes that extended through my mother back to my grandmother. Deedee would be my constant companion during the Hampton Roads years.

That any of that would happen is close to miraculous. Deedee had been one of a set of twins born prematurely. Deedee's lungs were not fully formed at birth and she and her twin each weighed less than two pounds. They spent their early weeks on a ventilator. Modern medicine thinks nothing of saving the lives of children born in this condition, but one can only imagine how challenging it would have been in the 1940s. The nurses at the hospital made up for any equipment deficiencies through the loving care that they gave to these two little infants. They even hand-made tiny clothes for Deedee. There was nothing to be found small enough for her in a regular baby store.

In the event, her twin died, but Deedee was somehow tough enough to pull through. It's likely that I knew little of this at the time, but I marvel today at the story of her survival and later history. From that inauspicious start, possessing only ill-formed lungs and dependent on a ventilator, Deedee grew up to be a talented singer, ultimately studying with a prominent voice coach, attending the New England Conservatory of Music, and becoming a lyric soprano good enough to have interned twice with the Santa Fe Opera Company.

Dad Ships Out to China

During the remainder of 1943 and throughout 1944, Dad served as a Port Signal Officer. In November 1944, he was promoted to the rank of captain and shortly thereafter assigned to the Office of Strategic Services or OSS. This organization was the forerunner of the CIA, and it played a role in the complicated dynamics of the war. Things moved quickly after that. While we children had no real concept of what was happening, we soon learned that he would be leaving for China. Suddenly, he was gone, performing intelligence duties on the other side of the world. My mother, little sister, and I were now alone. We would spend the next year and a half in our Hampton Roads apartment, apprehensively awaiting his return.

The year 1945 was pivotal in the war. The conflict had grown bigger and bigger and was reaching a crescendo. As we later learned, Dad was stationed in Kunming, China, where his duties included dealing with the Nationalist Chinese forces. The United States and its allies secured victory in Europe in May of the year, but the war continued in Asia. Dad would continue to be engaged there until it was over.

The period between the time that the United States declared war on Germany and the time that the Japanese surrendered to the United States and its allies in August 1945 was traumatic for virtually everyone on earth. The multifaceted conflicts that took place around the globe truly constituted a world war. All told, tens of millions of people, combatants and civilians alike, would die in foreign lands and waters, including hundreds of thousands of American soldiers and sailors.

As a child living in the United States, I was mostly sheltered from the war's trauma. I have few verifiable memories of the period. I seem to recall riding a tricycle, but that may simply mean that I've seen home movies showing me pedaling the trike on a local sidewalk. Nevertheless, looking back, I realize now how much my mother had to contend with, living in this strange new place with two young children, war tensions constantly present, with none of her New York friends and no husband around to lend a hand, unsure of when or even whether he would return.

Happily, it turned out all right. For his service, Dad had earned the American Theater Service Medal, the World War II Victory Medal, and the Asiatic Pacific Theater Medal with a Bronze Battle Star. But he returned from overseas, safe and sound. We would soon be on our way back home to Irvington!

The War Ended, We Return to West Clinton Avenue

My father was mustered out of the service in January 1946, and we returned to West Clinton Avenue shortly afterward. My first truly independent memories as a child, and my first memories of Irvington, date from that time. The war was over. The United States and its allies had won, in Europe and in Asia. Dad had been discharged from the Army. He was working once again at Wood Struthers & Winthrop. Mom had turned her attention to making a permanent home and raising a family in surroundings that were more congenial than a small, rented flat in a community mobilized for war. At last, we were in our own home!

My Grandmother's Place on Dows Lane

Grammy was now living in Irvington in a nearby carriage house. The carriage house was located on a short street in Irvington called Dows Lane. Dows Lane was once part of the great estate owned by David Dows, the distant relative who made millions dealing in grain a century earlier but who ultimately went bust. None of the Dows fortune ever filtered down to my grandmother or my mother. The Depression wiped out whatever wealth the Dowses might have had. The carriage house was all that was left. There was enough room there for Grammy, and for many years her own mother (my great-grandmother), Florence Dake Mattison. "Yanny" as we knew her, would live on to the age of 102.

Old as it was, the carriage house was nevertheless a marvelous structure. There was a cavernous room on the first

My grandmother Mary Dake Mattison Mairs (*family photo*)

floor with great sliding doors. Once upon a time, the Dows carriages were stored there. Upstairs was a small apartment, once occupied by a carriage man, now by the two women. Down below, under the carriage space, were several stalls where the Dows horses and a cow or two had been kept.

The greatest virtue of the carriage house was that it lay on a direct line between my school on Main Street and my home on West Clinton Avenue. I loved to drop in on my way home after school. To knock on Grammy's door was to be greeted by the cheeriest welcome that anyone could imagine and an invitation to join her for a cup of tea. I loved being in her company.

CHAPTER IV

Postwar Period

After the war ended, life slowly returned to normal. Lest anyone forget, every May 30, Memorial Day ceremonies would be held to honor those who had died and the sacrifices that others had made. Virtually the entire population of the Village of Irvington would gather at these ceremonies held in the village's appropriately renamed "Memorial Park." Veterans and "Gold Star Mothers," those who had lost a son or daughter in the war, were featured. Years later, as a member of the high school band, I participated in the day's moving and solemn events.

So, Americans would remember, and across the country we have held Memorial Day ceremonies ever since. But the country was also poised to break out of its wartime mentality. There was new work to be done, education to be resumed, life to be lived again.

For me, this change meant the new experience of going to school in the Irvington public schools.

My First Career Plan

Well, now. As a mature first grader, it was time to look ahead! What was I going to do for a living?

As far as I can recall, the first time I said anything on the subject was about then. My teacher was Miss Bouck, and she had invited me to submit an essay to an elementary school newspaper. This august publication consisted of six mimeographed sheets. There, amidst some twenty-odd contributions from other elementary school kids, appeared my article. It was entitled, simply, "Cowboys," and it read, in its entirety, as follows:

> Some day I am going to be a cowboy in the country of Canada with the cowboys and cowgals. But my mother and father call me a cow puncher. Deedee is coming to Canada too, but she can't be a cowboy. She can be a cow gal. I have a cowboy shirt. It was made by hand. It is a beautiful shirt. That is the end.
>
> Johnny Smith Grade I

Miss Bouck was sweet and pretty. All the boys in the class had a crush on her. Alas, she was engaged. By the end of first grade, she married her fiancé and broke our hearts.

JFSIII in a cowboy shirt, together with "cow gal" (*family photo*)

View of the Hudson River from our backyard (*family photo*)

My Fascination with Traffic on the Hudson River

As I have said, the view of the Hudson was spectacular from our house. Below the western property line, the land fell off, paralleling the long, gradual descent of the street, all the way down to the railroad tracks. Beyond was the river itself. With only a few trees here and there, one had a clear view of the water and the traffic that moved ceaselessly on it. Day and night, a continual parade of boats and ships moved up and down the river—commercial vessels, fishing boats, military vessels, pleasure craft, Hudson River Day Liners carrying passengers up from New York City for a day's outing, and many others. It was fascinating. I would sit on our back porch watching it all, mesmerized and full of wild wonderings. Where had all of these vessels come from? What were they doing here? Where were they going?

Old Gray Warriors on Their Way to Retirement

For me, of all the vessels on the Hudson River, the most intriguing were the "Liberty ships." These ships had been

Group of Liberty ships at the beginning of their lives in 1942, just launched from a South Portland, Maine, shipyard (*photo by Albert Freeman; courtesy of the Library of Congress*)

employed during World War II as transports. They had been built and launched almost overnight and commissioned during the war to carry American soldiers and war-fighting materiel from the United States to the conflicts in Europe, North Africa, and Asia.

Without their service, the United States could not have sent the millions of soldiers, marines, and airmen that were necessary to prevail overseas.

Now the war was over. The fighting had ended. The services of these vessels were no longer needed. There was no other present use for them. As a result, hundreds of Liberty ships were being retired. Many were being taken up the river to an anchorage at West Point.

Not all of these gutsy vessels had made it back from the war. Their work was dangerous, and they were attractive targets for Germany's submarines, also known as U-boats.

Tragically, many had been sunk, with their precious cargos of men and materiel. Yet here were the survivors! Great gray hulks of steel moving slowly now, some pulled by tugboats, up my very own river. They were not the sleek destroyers or the huge carriers bristling with aircraft on their decks. But they, too, were imposing. Veteran vessels that had crossed the dangerous Atlantic Ocean and made it to Europe and then come back, only to load up again and do it all over. Ships that had been in harm's way. Now those that survived were headed to a well-deserved retirement. They would be "put in mothballs" in case there might be some later use for them.

On this, their final voyage, I thrilled at seeing them. My boyish imagination constructed stories about them. We had had blackout exercises when my mother, sister, and I lived in Hampton Roads, a small taste of the wartime tensions we felt when living near that great military complex. As I would later come to understand, this was nothing like what London and Paris and, yes, the enemy cities of Dresden and Tokyo had been going through. But there was tension nevertheless and we practiced caution. Pearl Harbor had been the victim of a surprise bombing, and Germany's U-boats were operating off the Atlantic coast. Even though Virginia was thousands of miles from the real fighting, the authorities periodically required that precautions be taken against an attack. These included blackouts. At night, my mother would turn off the lights and pull down the shades in compliance.

Now back in Irvington, seeing these vessels on the move, I half-imagined that we were in a wartime situation again. Large military vessels were on the move. They probably had awesome firepower. They were our ships, but for an active imagination, it didn't take much to flip the scenario. What if the United States had lost and these were ships from the German *Wehrmacht*? On patrol. Right up the Hudson River. Right off the Village of Irvington! This sensation would occasionally come over me at night when all I could see was shadowy silhouettes of the ships and their red and green running lights. They were transformed by my mind's eye into German battleships and cruisers. It was a dangerous situation. We were under attack. We could be shelled at any time. A blackout was necessary, but we had somehow allowed the lights of our house to continue burning brightly. We were an obvious target. How could this be? What was to be done? Fortunately, I was on duty. To the undoubted amusement of my parents, I raced around the house, pulled down the shades, and turned out the lights. There. We were safe now.

Progress: Television and Beyond

Up until the time I was five, I had never seen a television set. Or even heard of one. But then, one of the families in our neighborhood got a TV. It was as big as a chest, but its screen was tiny, probably only eight inches wide by five inches high. The images weren't very good. They were in black-and-white, and they were grainy. There were only four commer-

Example of an early TV set (iStock, with permission)

cial channels—NBC, ABC, CBS, and Dumont. They didn't broadcast all day long, and the programming was limited. After they went off the air in the evening, all you could get on your screen was an unchanging geometric design known as a "test pattern."

When the new TV arrived, our neighbor's house became very popular overnight. The kids who lived there immediately became our best friends!

The children's program we watched most was the *Howdy Doody Show*. It featured a puppet named Howdy, a clown named Clarabelle, and a young woman dressed up as an Indian. She was called "Princess Summer Fall Winter Spring." All of the characters were overseen by a man called "Buffalo Bob." The story lines were trite, but we sat in our friends' living room each afternoon, packed together before the little screen, completely entranced, following the marvelous characters who now appeared in our world.

Back in the studio where the program was produced, a dozen or two kids would be gathered to watch the *Howdy Doody Show* live. They were surrogates, I guess, for the thousands—and, later, millions—of us who were sitting in our respective living rooms across the TV broadcasting area. They were referred to on the show as the "Peanut Gallery." (This phrase has a dubious history. It generally signifies an area of cheap seats, reserved for disfavored or boisterous people. On the *Howdy Doody Show*, it was an area cordoned off for the onlooking kids.)

Needless to say, Deedee and I agitated to get a TV for our house. After a long wait my parents finally bought one. Now Howdy Doody and his friends could come into our living room, too.

It was the beginning of an era, one in which virtually all of America would become addicted to the "tube." Today, we continue to be mesmerized by our TVs, though streaming on the internet has begun to replace broadcasting and our screens now come in a multitude of sizes, small to super-large. Ironically, we Americans now prize getting content directly through smartphones whose screens are even smaller than the one on which I watched Howdy Doody seventy-five years ago.

The television was only one of the new contrivances that came into our lives in the mid-1940s. Another was an electrically powered refrigerator, with a pump, refrigerant, and condensation coils. Can you imagine that? A real refrigerator! True, it was primitive compared to today's sleek and modern refrigerators. But it was quite a step up from the icebox that my mother had been relying on before. The icebox was just what it sounds like, a box, well-insulated to be sure, with a compartment above for a block of ice and a compartment below for the food, but still just a box. Aside from latches on the compartment doors, there were no moving parts. To keep it "going," an ice man would come with his truck once or twice a week and bring huge blocks of ice into the house with a set of iron tongs.

Progress was afoot in many other ways, as well.

In the 1940s, we had a single home telephone, and our phone number was Irvington 9-3241. There was no area code to worry about. On the phone, there were no numbered buttons. The phone was mostly for my parents to use, but I occasionally got permission to use it myself. When making a call, I picked up the handset and asked an operator, who was readily available, to get the number for me.

Although our number was distinct, the phone line that we were on was not. It was a party line, one that was shared with other families in the neighborhood. Sometimes, when I picked up the phone to make a call, one of our neighbors would already be on the line having a conversation with someone else. When that happened, I would have to apologize, put down the phone, and wait until the party line was free. Or, I suppose, I could have stayed on and listened to what they were saying! Conversely, if I was having a phone conversation, there was no guarantee that someone else wouldn't be listening in.

For obvious reasons, there wasn't much privacy on our party line! In a few years, though, the system changed, as did our phone number. It was now Lyric 1-8356, expressed as LY 1-8356. We were no longer on a party line, so we got our privacy back. As a family, that is. There was still just one phone line for everyone in our family. We all had to use it, and my parents were in charge. The mobile phone hadn't been invented yet, and I didn't have the luxury of being able to call anyone I wanted whenever I wanted.

New technology also invaded the shoe store. My mother favored the Thom McAn brand of shoes for me and my siblings. When I outgrew a pair of shoes, she and I would drive over to the Thom McAn store in White Plains, and I would try on a new pair. The store featured a piece of equipment called a "fluoroscope." It looked like a weighing scale that you had to put your feet in instead of on. In reality, it was an x-ray machine, minus the protections against extraneous radiation that true x-ray machines have. I would stand up to it, put my feet though a slot in the bottom, and look down at them through a viewing scope on the top. There, in eerie green and white, I could see the bones of my feet and a faint outline of the sole of the shoe. If there was room between the two, the salesman would pronounce that the shoe "fit," and out the store I would go with a new pair.

No one in that day seemed to be aware of the potentially harmful effects of the radiation that was emanating from the machine. My mother and I certainly weren't. I don't think I was actually harmed, but Lord knows what effects those fluoroscopes may have had on a whole generation of shoe buyers like me.

There was also progress in our ability to get places. Until the late 1940s, if you lived in Irvington and wanted to cross the river, either you went on foot, taking a small passenger ferry to Piermont on the other side, or you drove a long distance down along the river to New York City and crossed over on the George Washington Bridge. It was time for a change. New York State finally built a road system called the "Thruway" that connected New York City with the city of Buffalo in the western part of the state. The Thruway project involved building a massive bridge called the "Tappan Zee Bridge." I regularly went down to riverside to watch its construction.

In short, there was great progress in this period, and it took many forms. Of all of them, though, television was the one that had the greatest impact. It just took a little getting used to, as the following anecdote reflects.

The Today Show: "Hey, I Know Him!"

In 1952, NBC created a morning television program called *The Today Show*. Broadcast in black-and-white like everything else in those days, it was a staple of news and human-interest programming for adults. One of the first hosts of the program was Frank Blair. Mr. Blair was a neighbor of ours. He lived just down West Clinton Avenue on Ardsley Terrace. I knew Mr. Blair from seeing him in the neighborhood. There, in the flesh, he seemed real enough. One morning, though, I was watching TV and saw *The Today Show* for the first time. Frank Blair happened to be presiding. All of a sudden, there he was, not our neighbor now but rather a disembodied image. After recovering from my surprise, I shouted, "Hey, I know him!" But it was still hard to believe. It took me a while to reconcile the real Frank Blair, the one I knew, and the one now appearing in our living room, flickering in grainy black-and-white.

CHAPTER V

Family Life

My Family Grows

During the 1940s and in early 1950, I grew taller and leaner. Every now and then, I had a kid-type malady, but generally I was very healthy.

Along the way, my family grew, too.

I've already described the grit that enabled my sister Deedee to survive her premature birth in 1943. She continued to need it. In our early years, I teased her unmercifully. Not surprisingly, my teasing would make her very angry. She took it and took it for a while. Then one day she had had enough. I said something to get her goat and suddenly she flew at me. I had never seen her so determined. It was a painful encounter, and I came off second best. I stopped teasing her then and there. We have been best friends ever since.

Later, following her singing career, Deedee worked as Executive Assistant to Rudolf Bing, the Director of the Metropolitan Opera Company, then moved to Philadelphia to serve in the same capacity for John Delancey, the Director of the Curtis School of Music. Over the years that have passed since then, she has been the cheeriest member of our family. She greets us on the first of each month with an uplifting message and, as family achievements come along, celebrates them with a spirited note of congratulations.

My brother, David Maulsby Smith, arrived in 1946. David was easily the most affable member of our family. He was always saying funny things, and his humor was contagious. Our family would occasionally go out for Sunday dinner at the Schrafft's restaurant in Eastchester. No sooner had we been seated than he would crack a joke. We would all start laughing, including my mother and father, and by the time our meal arrived we would be in stitches. Diners at neighboring tables would look at us in wonderment. David's ability to charm would serve him well throughout his life. He became the voice of the morning show of WNLK, the radio station of Norwalk, Connecticut, and later the host of a regular cable TV show called the *Fairfield Exchange*. To this day, well after his retirement, former fans still hasten to greet him when he is out in public. He is now an election official in his hometown of Easton, Connecticut, and performs wedding ceremonies on the side.

My younger sister, Linda Mairs Smith, came along in January 1950. When my mother was pregnant with her, Deedee, David, and I would take turns feeling Linny move inside her. Her energy in there was a harbinger of the active young woman she would become. One of the sweetest and most solicitous people in the world, Linny is also one of the brightest. After going away to boarding school, Linny enrolled at Wellesley College. Two years later, she transferred and became one of the first women to attend Yale University as an undergraduate. Not content with these achievements, she went to work at the U.S. Department of Housing and Urban Development. Later, after earning an MBA at Wharton, she went into banking and then worked as a development officer for several charitable organizations.

THERE IS A funny story about Linda that occurred much later than the rest of the stories in this book. Because I have talked about early TV, though, it is too good to pass up. I call it:

The Beatles Take America by Storm

Quite a few people in the early television industry lived in Irvington, including some who never appeared in front of a camera. Among them was a man named Thayer Drake. Mr. Drake was the general legal counsel of the Columbia Broadcasting Service, better known as CBS.

Among CBS's lineup of programs was a Sunday evening variety show called the *Ed Sullivan Show*. It was one of the longest-running programs in the history of television. Sullivan always had an eye out for new talent, and in the early 1960s he happened to be in England and to see a performance by a new group called the Beatles. He signed them up and on February 9, 1964, introduced them to the American public on his show. It was a big occasion. Tickets to be in the live audience at the Ed Sullivan Theater were scarce. But because of his position, Mr. Drake had a pair. Luckily for my sister Linda, he gave them to his daughter, who was Linda's best friend. The tickets were for first-row seats.

The Beatles' appearance has been called a milestone in American pop culture. To say the least, it was a frenzied event. Teenage girls, especially, had gone mad for the Beatles. CBS made the most of it. The theater was packed and throbbing with anticipation. A close-up shot of John Lennon during the show included a caption that read, "SORRY GIRLS, HE'S MARRIED!" The teenagers lucky enough to be in the theater that night were beside themselves, jumping up and down and screaming. My family and I watched from our living room, along with more than seventy million other television viewers. As the camera panned the audience, we saw a familiar figure. It was not the suave host Ted Mack. It was not the cool newscaster Frank Blair. It was not even my warm, highly educated, and super-accomplished sister, the person that most people know today. It was her younger self, enjoying her youthfulness, screaming with excitement like the rest, having the time of her life on national television.

THERE IS A lot more that I could say about my sisters and brother, about the people they married and about the families they have raised. Perhaps the most important thing to say here is that we are still very close. To this day, we have been not just siblings but the dearest of friends.

Cream Rises to the Top

In the late 1940s, my mother usually didn't shop for milk or cream. Instead, we had a milk box outside the kitchen door. Every day or two a milkman would deliver two quarts of milk, depositing them in the box. The milk that we ordered was whole milk, not the 1 percent or 2 percent varieties that predominate today. Moreover, it was not homogenized. Each bottle would have a top layer of cream that had separated from the milk below. If my mother wanted cream, she didn't have to buy it separately. She simply poured it off from the top.

Butter was a different story. You needed to buy that by itself. If you were cost conscious, you didn't buy butter at all. You bought margarine instead. Butter and margarine were quite distinct. There was no confusing one with the other. The powerful dairy lobby saw to that. If you bought a pound or a stick of butter, it looked like butter, with a soft yellowish color. If you bought margarine, you bought something that was pale white. By virtue of federal law, margarine could not be sold looking like butter. So, if you wanted to put butter on your toast, you had to buy the real thing.

Faced with this disadvantage, what were the manufacturers of margarine to do? Obey the letter of the law, of course, but find a way to innovate around it. The solution? Sell the margarine wrapped in a strong but malleable clear plastic bag and put a small, button-sized capsule of yellow food dye inside, along with the margarine.

It worked like a charm. My mother would buy bags of margarine like this, storing them initially in the refrigerator. When we needed more "butter," she would take one of the bags out of the fridge, allow it to warm up a little, and then give it to me. It would still be securely enclosed on all sides by the plastic casing. My job was to take the bag, burst the little yellow capsule inside with my thumb, then squeeze and knead the bag until the dye was uniformly distributed throughout. I usually sat on a stool in the kitchen doing this while she cooked dinner. It was a mindless but pleasurable chore. I remember those moments fondly. I would sit there, chatting with her about any subject that might come up, squeezing and kneading the margarine all the while. I found that the time passed quickly. It was a Zen-like activity. Before long, the margarine had turned into a warm pale-yellow color. Mission accomplished. We now had a week's worth of "butter."

Leadership Training at the Yellow Brick Pile

Our house in Irvington was a rectangular structure. The core of the house was made of yellow bricks painted white. Unpainted bricks, awaiting the construction of the wing that would be added to the core once my parents could afford it, were piled in a corner of the yard. They would be used in due course. But since the wing never happened, the brick pile stood off to one side, unused, year after year.

My sister Deedee and I rediscovered the brick pile when our family moved back to Irvington from our wartime apartment in Hampton Roads, Virginia.

The bricks were of a high quality, clean and solid, and there were lots of them. They were perfect for kids to use to build things. Unlike today's Lego sets, they came with no instructions prescribing how they should be put together. They were just there, waiting for us to come along and do something with them. Our imaginations were the only guide, and they were unfettered. So, we created everything imaginable: castles and moats and forts, of course, and more mundane structures like houses, highways, walls, and tunnels. Neighborhood kids would hear about what we were doing and come over and ask to play with us. Sometimes there would be three or four other kids working with us, and multiple projects would be going on at once. It wasn't necessarily the safest play environment. Every now and then a structure got too tall. Six layers, seven layers, then eight layers high. Too much! Without adequate support, it would begin to teeter back and forth. "Watch out!" someone would cry, just as the bricks began to fall. If you weren't careful, they crashed on you. It helped if one of us supervised the activity. I often found myself in that role. At first, I was very bossy. "Do it this way," I would dictate. "You can't build that high without a broader base," I would say with great authority. I was entitled to speak that way, I thought. It was, after all, *my* brick pile. My instructions, however, were not always well received. After a while, I began to realize that things went better if I eased up on telling people what to do. Someone else might have a good idea. Even if I thought my idea was better, projects went more smoothly when there was give-and-take.

Many years later, when I was in Officer Candidate School preparing to become a naval officer, our instructors emphasized that leadership is "getting things done through other people," not ordering them around. The message resonated for me. Thanks to a discarded pile of bricks in my Irvington backyard, I had started to learn it as a kid.

Sledding on West Clinton

West Clinton Avenue was ideal for sledding. Consider the topography: Starting from its intersection with Broadway, the road first rose briefly. Then, from that higher elevation, it sloped down, past the old Murray farm, across the New York Aqueduct, past our house halfway along, and on down to the railroad tracks at the bottom. The drop in elevation from top to bottom was considerable.

In the winter our street amounted to a toboggan run, a half mile of greased lightning.

Siblings on a Flexible Flyer—unsafe at any speed (*family photo*)

To my delight, the winters of the 1940s produced lots of snow each year. I'm probably not the most objective observer, but I knew that after a snowstorm, if you got out there before the town plow came through and destroyed the fun, West Clinton was the greatest sled run in the land, easily surpassing anything that Lake Placid and the Winter Olympic Games had to offer. You would pull your Flexible Flyer up the snow-covered street, turn around, grab the rope, hop on, and let her rip, either lying on your belly or sitting up and steering with your feet.

Cars used chains on their tires back then—the snow tire and the radial hadn't been invented yet. Using chains, cars were able to negotiate the grade and get up the hill. Fortunately, the chained tires didn't rip up the snow too much. Mostly they packed it firmer, making the conditions even better.

The fastest portion of the run was the bottom half, beginning at our driveway. We generally started at that point. As long as no car was coming, the coast was clear. A running start or a short push and you were off. In a few seconds you were going at a thrilling clip.

We had lots of good times sledding with our neighborhood friends. After a run we would race back up the hill to our place, jump on our sleds, and head down once again. Two people on the sled would add weight and make the sled go faster. If you wanted to make a controlled run, you could scud your feet alongside to keep the sled from going too fast. Otherwise, it was full speed ahead. The faster you went the better.

Of course, there was the matter of braking. You had to use your feet for this, but if you were in a sitting position, you also needed your feet for steering. You couldn't do both. As the sled moved faster and faster, you had to decide—steer or brake. If you were bold or foolish enough to keep your feet up all the way, your sled would hurtle down the grade and pick up a terrific amount of momentum. This wasn't necessarily the best decision to make. At the bottom, the street ended abruptly at a wooden barricade. The barricade was there to prevent vehicles from proceeding onto the railroad's right-of-way and hitting the tracks that lay just beyond. For that matter, it could also stop sleds that were out of control.

I remember an incident involving Deedee. She had a friend with her on her sled. There was plenty of snow. The street hadn't been plowed. The snow on West Clinton was packed and ready. The surface was perfect for speed. New sledding records would be set. The Olympic Torch had been lit!

So off went Deedee and her friend. Carefree, they headed downhill, going slowly at first. Deedee was steering. Her feet were on the steering bar. Soon they were moving lickety-split. I had finished a run earlier and was pulling my sled uphill when they passed me going the other way. Their momentum was increasing. They were going faster and faster. Wow! I didn't know she could go that fast. Was this a new Olympic record in the making? I watched in amazement. The sled was getting close to the bottom of the street. It was going too fast now. My amazement turned into horror. The wooden barricade was just ahead. Deedee took her feet off the steering bar and tried to use them to brake. She even tried to use her hands, dangerously gripping the runners of the sled where they touched the snow. Too late. At the last moment, she put her feet up protectively.

Crash!

I'm not sure what or who came out worse, the barricade or the sledders. At least one of its wooden members was broken, but otherwise the barricade held. Deedee and her friend were hurt, but they had set a record of some sort. In any event, they had been lucky. The barricade had prevented them from sailing through to the tracks and the high voltage "third rail" beyond.

The Joy of Christmas—and of Waiting for It

Not surprisingly, Christmas was my favorite holiday. The prospect of getting presents was undoubtedly one of its principal virtues, but I also liked the run-up to the big day. This story is about how my family and I celebrated it.

First, a little background:

My family attended St. Barnabas, the Episcopal church in Irvington where I was baptized. I wasn't too big on Sunday School. I could sing, though. When I was nine, I joined the church's boy choir. Being in the boy choir meant rehearsing once a week and attending the adult service at 11 o'clock almost every Sunday. It was a big-time commitment, but I loved the music. My choir experience began a life-long love of music of all kinds. And I loved the camaraderie. A lot of my buddies were in the choir. It was like a club. Our "club leader" was Mr. McLaughlin, the organist and choir master. He was an excellent musician, and he could be serious, but he had a great sense of humor and knew how to use it to keep us interested. We shared in-jokes together. For example, occasionally during a service he would take a ridiculous pop song and turn it into a serious-sounding piece of meditative music on the organ. One of my favorites was a transformed version of the 1940s' hit "Yes, We Have No Bananas." He converted it so convincingly that the congregation had no idea of what was going on. Only he—and we—were in on the joke. Kneeling reverently in our stations on either side of the altar during the church service, we struggled to keep straight faces. Being in the choir also meant having an outing. We went to the Ringling Brothers Barnum & Bailey Circus in Madison Square Garden every year, with Mr. McLaughlin and a handful of parents.

And we were paid for our singing labors! Not much, it's true, but our needs were minimal.

Beneath my choir experience, though, was something of greater seriousness and longer-lasting impact: the running ritual of the liturgical calendar. This is a specialized calendar marking the landmark events of the Christian story as they are commemorated during the year. Easter and Christmas are the highlights. Several important events lead up to Christmas. Annunciation Sunday celebrates the moment when, in the belief of Christians, the Archangel Gabriel announces to Mary that she will soon bear a child. This day is followed by a series of Sundays called Advent, during which Christians wait expectantly for the birth of Jesus. Advent is filled with hopeful songs. "Come, O Come, Emmanuel," which is sung in a minor musical key, was one of my favorites.

Of course, outside of church you didn't really need Advent to tell you that Christmas Day was coming. There was plenty of advertising and Christmas music to alert the unwary. Whatever your faith, department store Santas and schoolroom decorations made sure that you were brought to a fever pitch of anticipation.

During my early childhood, as Christmas Day approached, its imminence was further heralded by the arrival of my father's aunt—and thus my great aunt—Miss Mary Maulsby. We called her "Yarry." Yarry lived in Frederick, Maryland, but every Christmas she came up to visit us in Irvington. She was a great character. We loved her. When she came through the door, she automatically became the leader of us kids. The energy level of the household went up exponentially. With mounting expectations, we were beside ourselves.

One of Yarry's roles was to distract us on Christmas Eve so that my father and mother could set up the living room and have it ready for the following morning. We had a tree in the living room, but even the day before Christmas it wasn't

lit. Its sole decoration might have been the chains we children had fashioned out of colored paper and paste in school.
Otherwise, the room looked just the way it did any other day
of the year. At bedtime, without any fanfare, the living room
door would close. It would be locked for good measure. And
it would not open again until the morning.

During the years that Yarry was there, Christmas morning would begin with a bang. Just as we were beginning to
wake up, she would burst into our bedrooms, still dressed in
her nightgown, singing at the top of her lungs a simple but
catchy set of lyrics:

> It's Christmas Day in the morning.
> Christmas Day in the morning.
> Christmas Day in the morning.
> The work's most done!
>
> Where are the Hebrew children?
> Oh, where are the Hebrew children?
> Where are the Hebrew children?
> Safe in the Promised Land!
>
> And where is baby Jesus?
> Where is baby Jesus?
> Where is baby Jesus?
> Safe in the Promised Land!

Pretty soon, she had us up and singing, too. There were
more verses, I'm sure, but the lyrics were simple enough. The
beat was infectious, and we were soon marching around in
our pj's making a holy racket.

Whatever my parents may have thought of this performance, they never told us to tone it down or intervened to
stop it. Yarry was always careful to keep the mayhem in and
around our bedrooms. We were never steered down toward

Mary Maulsby, the irrepressible "Yarry" (*family photo*)

the living room to demand entrance. After a while we exhausted ourselves. Whatever lay behind the now-locked living room door would have to wait.

To make matters worse, at least in the early years there were no stockings to open at that point. Dad and Mom believed in keeping the suspense going. It was time for breakfast. A wonderful breakfast, to be sure, but there were no toys—or candies or apples or lumps of coal—to enjoy while we were waiting for the main event.

The wait became excruciating. The rule was that our Christmas celebration would not begin until Grammy arrived. She would walk over to our house around 8:30 or 9:00, bearing her all-important gift book. This was a register of who gave what to whom, carefully recorded by Grammy as each present was given. The big presents all needed to be marked down so that we could be sure of who our benefactors were and be appropriately grateful. A thank-you note would be required later. The waiting was quite a discipline, and the patience it required was almost inhuman.

When the dear lady finally arrived, Dad would slip into the living room to turn everything on. And then, at last, the door would open, revealing a magical scene—the tree beautifully decorated, with lights on, electric train running beneath, and presents all about. It was almost enough to make us forget the wait!

But the waiting was part of the message.

Now, years later, I have become a father and a grandfather. Raising our own children, Susan and I abandoned the notion of a super-suspenseful Christmas. Like most folks today, we made the stockings available first thing on Christmas Day, as soon as our boys came downstairs. As time passed, our present giving took place earlier and earlier in the holiday season. In some ways, this practice has been necessary. Family schedules are more complicated in the twenty-first century. We give our loved ones presents when we can be together. For still further reasons, it has also been desirable. Giving gifts gradually, instead of in rush, all at one time, has meant that the recipients can have a greater appreciation for each gift received. And can acknowledge it more fully. There is a case for doing it that way.

Still, I miss the waiting. Though I became a Unitarian Universalist long ago, thinking of Jesus now as an extraordinary prophet and teacher and not uniquely the son of God, I miss the progression of liturgical events that is celebrated through the Christian calendar. That includes Advent and Christmas. In my view, they are best understood as working together. The waiting and the waited for. Without Advent, Christmas is in danger of becoming a series of rolling events, with presents at every stop. With Advent, with the waiting, with the anticipation that some form of Emmanuel is coming, whatever our religious tradition, we can better appreciate the joy that Christmas brings when it finally arrives.

Of Cats, Vises, and Birthdays

Once, as an eight- or nine-year-old, I flew to Rochester, New York, to visit a friend. As fate would have it, his family's cat had just produced a litter. Predictably, I fell in love with one of the kittens and wanted to take it back home. It was an early test of my nascent advocacy skills. The family helped me place a long-distance call—something that was new in my experience—back to Irvington. After an impassioned plea to my mother, I won my case. Two days later, when I flew back home, I had a shoe box with me and in it was the kitten.

Rusty became a fixture in our home. She got along with our dogs. She was my constant companion. But she must also have found male cat companionship, too, because one day she produced a litter of her own! It wasn't clear at first what was going on. She would disappear into the cellar from time to time, coming back up for a meal each evening. Then one day she didn't reappear. We searched for her and discov-

Rusty with kittens
(*family photo*)

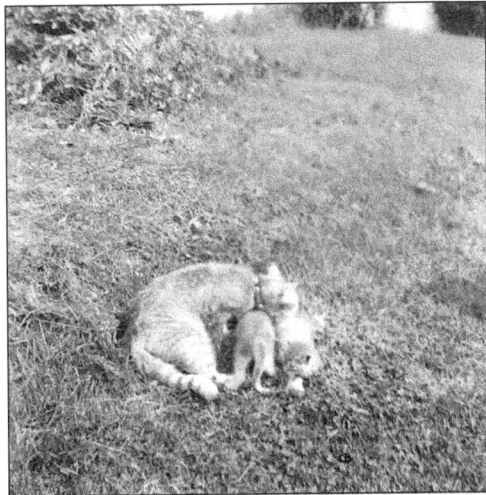

ered that the cat population of 15 West Clinton Avenue had just grown by five. It was a joyous event for me but slightly less joyous for my parents. What would we do with the new kittens?

Strangely enough, the solution would be related to Canal Street, a historic street in the lower Manhattan part of New York City. Canal Street was laid out in the colonial days when the Dutch ruled New York. By the 1940s, however, it had become a street of wholesalers, merchandising everything from electrical devices to toothbrushes to tools. Canal Street was not far from New York's Financial District, where my father worked, and at lunchtime he would occasionally go there to browse.

When Dad found something that he liked, he didn't go halfway and buy just one or two. No, he would buy a bunch. Why stop with one or two when he could get the pleasure of a good deal on a lot of them? This was, after all, a wholesaler's paradise. You usually bought things in bulk. So, one day, when he came across a particularly attractive small shop vise that could be used for home woodworking, he did what any smart shopper would do in such a circumstance: He bought a half dozen of them. On his return from work that evening, he triumphally produced his haul. "One is for you, Johnny," he said, "and I could use one myself." My mother was in shock. "Right," she said, "but what about the other four?"

So, you could say that we had a surplus. Two surpluses, actually: one of kittens and one of vises.

Come September, however, a solution came into view.

Deedee would have a birthday on the fifteenth of the month and I would have one on the twenty-fourth. She would have a birthday party attended by all of her friends; I would have one attended by mine. What would make for unforgettable party prizes or favors for our friends? Nice cuddly kittens, of course, or in some cases a neat turn-the-handle-and-squeeze-something-tight vise. Bingo! The novel party prizes were duly handed out. The kids went away thrilled. Our overstocks were depleted.

Problem solved.

History does not record how the parents of the party attendees felt when their kids came home with their prizes.

.

CHAPTER VI

School Days

From 1946 to 1956 I attended Irvington's public schools from kindergarten to the end of tenth grade. I liked school and turned out to be pretty good at it. Of course, not everything was rosy. As with most of us, my early school years were a time for growing up. Some lessons came from the classroom, where academics were taught, and some from the playground, where life was taught. Here are some memories that stand out.

Pennybridge—Old Name, Old School

In the third and fourth grades, my classmates and I were bussed to an old school building in the northeast section of the Irvington School District. The Pennybridge School was built in 1905, not far from where a wooden bridge was operated in colonial times. The bridge was used to bring cattle raised in the countryside into New York City. The charge for each person or head of cattle that crossed the bridge was a penny. Naturally, the bridge was called the "Penny Bridge" and the area in which it was located picked up the name as well.

The Pennybridge School was showing its age when we were there, and it has long since stopped being a school. The "gym" was little more than the basement of the building, with support columns throughout. When we played down there—in the winter there was no place else—the columns added an interesting dimension. In games of kickball or dodgeball, the balls would carom off the columns, almost like a pinball machine, adding unpredictability—and fun— to the game.

Riding on the Aqueduct

When I reached fifth grade, I was back attending classes at the Main Street School. I had a serviceable bicycle by that time, and though the school bus was still an option, I greatly preferred to ride my bike to school. My route was a dirt trail between West Clinton Avenue and Main Street, ending right at the entrance to the school, that ran on top of something called the Croton Aqueduct.

Have you ever wondered how a huge city like New York gets the water it needs each day for drinking purposes and for fighting fires, cleaning streets, flushing toilets, and so on? The answer is a huge underground tunnel called an aqueduct that carries water from rivers and reservoirs way to the city's north and west down into the city itself. The aqueduct delivers roughly a billion gallons of water to millions of thirsty New Yorkers every single day.

The aqueduct that I rode on top of begins at a series of lakes near Croton-on-Hudson, New York. The Croton Aqueduct then travels south through the Hudson River Valley towns and villages that lie in its path, including Irvington, until it winds up at reservoirs in New York City. It was built in the nineteenth century, with improvements being added over the years since. As I later came to appreciate, it is an amazing feat of engineering. The aqueduct relies on gravity, not pumps, to move the water down from the Croton lakes to the big city. This means that its path must be smooth and on an even decline. It may encounter hills and valleys along the way, but it doesn't have the luxury of going up over the high points or of dipping down into the valleys. It must be straight, sloping downward the whole way.

While the aqueduct runs mostly underground, when it reaches a valley, adjustments need to be made. These involve the construction of earthen bridges or abutments based on the floor of the valley and built as high as needed to support the tunnel and maintain the gentle downward slope. If the valley is deep, the height of the abutment can be substantial, and its sides can be steep.

For the most part, my route to school followed flat terrain. The aqueduct's right-of-way consisted generally of a long, fifteen-yard-wide strip of meadow with a well-worn dirt track running along in the middle.

It was easy walking and easy riding, perfect for pedestrians and for bike riders like me! Except for when the path crossed a road, there were no cars. I might encounter a person or two walking along the way, but for the most part I had the aqueduct to myself. Just me on top and millions of

Path along the top of the Croton Aqueduct (*photo by Beyond My Ken – Own Work; courtesy of Wikimedia Commons*)

gallons of water flowing silently through the tunnel below. Pedaling along, I experienced a great sense of freedom.

There was one stretch, though, that sometimes gave me pause. This was the part of the aqueduct that crossed a valley about two-thirds of the way along my route. The valley certainly provided a challenge for the aqueduct's engineers. It was roughly fifty feet deep and from one side to the other was about as wide as a football field is long. The earthen abutment that had been built up from the valley floor to support the aqueduct was high enough and long enough to completely encompass the aqueduct's tunnel and permit pedestrians and bicyclists to cross the pathway on top. Down below, there was a road that crossed the aqueduct's path, running through a specially constructed tunnel underneath.

As you approached the pathway above, it became very narrow. The meadow dropped off, giving way to sides that

Station Road tunnel under the Croton Aqueduct; my bike route was fifty feet overhead (*photo by Beyond My Ken – Own Work; courtesy of Wikimedia Commons*)

were steep. There were no railings or fences to keep you from going up to the edge or—for that matter—over it. Occasionally, for the thrill of it, I would get off my bike and look down to see the valley floor below. In the mind of an eleven-year-old, this was great fun. But there were days of blustery weather that weren't as much fun, days that didn't invite me to get off my bike and look around. Sometimes it would be snowing, and sometimes a wintery wind would come sweeping up the sides of the abutment and slam into me. On those occasions, it was all I could do to keep the bike upright and on the path. There was no dawdling to be done. I would put my head down, pedaling as hard as I could, and be thankful when I got to the other side. Going to school those days was an adventure.

Stern Mrs. Bishop

Every school experience needs a stern taskmaster with a warm heart, and Mrs. Bishop was ours. She taught English in the seventh and eighth grades. She was convinced that good writing required a good sense of sentence structure. To teach structure, she taught us how to diagram sentences. Diagramming a sentence with only a subject and a verb— "Mary runs"—was simple: subject at one end of the horizontal diagram line, intransitive verb at the other, with a vertical bar in between. For a transitive sentence, one where the verb was affecting an object—"Johnny hit the ball"—the verb side of the line was extended, a forward-slanting line was added, and the object being affected appeared on the horizontal line following the slanted line. Adjectives and adverbs were appended on slanted lines running up from below into the word they modified. For every kind of sentence, there was a diagram that revealed its bones, what went with what. No sentence was too complicated to be diagrammed.

The challenge of diagramming opened new vistas for me.

For the first time, I saw how the words worked together in a sentence. If the sentence went on and on and was loaded with too many adjectives and adverbs, you could strip it down to the basics. What was the author really saying?

We didn't diagram paragraphs, but after learning the discipline of sentence diagramming, it was easier for me to consider how the sentences related to one another in a paragraph. Did the paragraph contain something worth considering and did the sentences work together in an orderly fashion to make it clear?

While I had no appreciation of it at the time, mastering the simple exercise of sentence diagramming was an important step in my education. It was the beginning of learning how to write well. Even more fundamentally, it was the beginning of learning how to think well. Only after the passage of many years did I come to a full appreciation of how big a gift Mrs. Bishop had given me.

Chalk Flies in Math Class

Math doesn't come easily to many people. Happily, I was an exception. There was something beautiful about its architecture for me. In that respect, I was a nerd. I liked math class, and I liked Mr. Ludington, the man who taught it in middle school.

Mr. Ludington was devoted to his subject. And he was something of a character. You either found that entertaining, as I did, or thought it something to ridicule, as some of my classmates did. He often lectured at the blackboard, writing with a piece of chalk, with his back turned to the class. As he wrote his equations, there were opportunities for students to make fun of him, literally behind his back. For a few students, the urge to make fun was irresistible. Occasionally, their wisecracking went over the top. On those occasions, Mr. Ludington was not without means for dealing with it. He might be in the middle of writing a mathe-matical expression on the board when someone would make a disruptive remark. Suddenly, he would whirl around, a florid expression on his face, and send the chalk in his hand flying like a missile at the offending student. His accuracy was remarkable. He rarely missed the intended target. This had a sobering effect on the offender—and all of us, too—at least for a while. The room would go silent, and instruction would continue without further disruption.

Whether launching chalk projectiles at your students is orthodox pedagogy or an effective long-term strategy for classroom control may be debated. As far as I am aware, the occasional incidents never became the subject of parental complaints or school board inquiries. They did, however, add to the lore about the unusual Mr. Ludington.

Life on the Playground

Lunchtime and recess. These were times when the edu-cation process moved into the lunchroom or out onto the playground. For the most part, they were happy times. My friends and I were glad to be at lunch or outside playing. Who wasn't ready for a break from the classroom? And the breaks served an important purpose. Socialization is part of the school experience, getting to know people different from yourself and learning how to get along with them. The inter-changes outside of the classroom did just that.

In the real world, though, these breaks had their down-sides. Cliques formed. Like people stuck with like people. To be different ran the risk of being shunned. Or being bul-lied. God forbid that you would try to sit down at the wrong table. It could be tough out there.

I was a thin kid in junior high school. And, as previously mentioned, I was regarded as a nerd. I hung out mostly with other kids who were doing well academically. The brainiacs, we were sometimes called. And names a lot worse than that. We were definitely not part of the in-crowd, the popular girls, the bigger and more mature boys, the jocks. To avoid the ridicule, we stuck with "our own kind." Obviously, this didn't look very much like the socialization that was supposed to happen outside the classroom.

I remember the leader of the jock group. He was a big kid and an excellent athlete. For the purpose of this story, I'll call him Mark. In private, one-on-one encounters, he was a nice enough person. I respected his ability on the baseball field. He seemed to respect my success in the classroom. Outside, in group settings, he became a different person. With the other bigger boys, he would make fun of us nerds, leading the taunts that would be shouted in our direction.

One day, however, a remarkable thing happened. It was winter, and we were outdoors at recess. It had snowed the night before. The snow was the wet, heavy kind that is good for making snowballs. As usual, we students were arrayed in our respective cliques. Soon the inevitable snowballing began. Within a given group, it was mostly in fun, but the snowballing between groups had a completely different character. The bigger kids were on higher ground and began pommeling those of us in the nerd group. They were laughing now, and the name-calling was intense. Snowballs were raining down on us, and it felt as though we could do nothing to stop it.

Then, a well-packed snowball hit me squarely in the face. Boy, did that sting! I was momentarily stunned. But then I became angry. You could say that I "lost it." I could think of nothing else but going after the kids that were harassing us. As I ran up the hill toward them, I was singled out as a target and got hit again and again. This only made me madder. I grabbed a handful of snow and, as poorly packed as it was, threw it in their direction. Suddenly I was in front of Mark. Whatever fear I might normally have felt was by this time overcome by rage. Picking up more snow, packing it on the fly, and throwing it at Mark became an obsession. I'm sure that he had never seen anything like it. He backed up a step and I rushed at him, now with my fists. In another setting, he might have whipped me, but there was no stopping me now. We fell down in the snow, with me punching him and Mark trying to protect himself from the unexpected assault. Amazingly, I was on the offensive and he was on the defensive. I was exultant.

Our confrontation must not have lasted too long. After a few minutes, some kids came over and pulled us apart. Across the playground, the snowballing came to an end. We had created a small spectacle and the other kids, whatever their group, had gathered to watch. Mark and I sat in the snow catching our breath. I could hear excited talk around us, but neither of us spoke a word. I had a bloody lip, and Mark's face was red and swollen. The recess bell rang at that point. It was time to go back in. I put some snow on my lip, wiped my face, and, along with everyone else, went back to class.

Talk about the snowball fight continued for a few days afterward, but soon enough it died down. No disciplinary repercussions ensued, and in the weeks that followed life went on in the schoolyard as before. Some things changed, though. I had proven to myself and my classmates that I was physically capable and not to be messed with. I had a new confidence in myself. The taunting of the nerds died down.

And, in time, Mark and I became friends.

Channeling Benny Goodman

After my years as a boy soprano at the St. Barnabas Episcopal Church, I became intrigued by the clarinet. This undoubtedly had something to do with a record that my parents owned featuring a clarinet player by the name of Benny

Goodman. Goodman was famous in the 1930s and 1940s for the highly rhythmic music he and his band played. As I later learned, the music was called "swing" and the young adults of the period—including my mother and father—loved to dance to it.

In 1938, the Benny Goodman Band had become so popular that Carnegie Hall in New York City invited Goodman and his band to play there. This was a departure for that venue. Carnegie Hall almost always featured orchestras and artists playing highbrow classical music. That Goodman and fellow musicians, like Lionel Hampton on the vibraphone, Harry James on the trumpet, and Gene Krupa on the drums, were going to play this new, swinging style of music in that staid hall was big news. They didn't disappoint. Their performance was a wild success. Goodman's clarinet soared over hits like "Sing, Sing, Sing" and Krupa's drumming provided an irresistible beat. Many of the patrons left their seats to dance in the aisles.

Goodman's performance took place well before I was born but, listening to the record twelve years later, I was drawn in to imagining what it must have been like. I loved the record and played it over and over again. Wouldn't it be great, I thought, if I could play an instrument like that?

When I got to fifth grade, my opportunity came. The school offered my classmates and me the chance to learn an instrument. I didn't give it a minute's thought. I was already sold. "I want a clarinet!" I said.

I enjoyed learning to play the instrument and over the next several years took regular lessons. I worked hard at it, but it wasn't really work. It was fun. My parents led by example. Dad had taken up the flute. Mom played the piano a little and later took up the flute herself. (She got very good at it and soon, to Dad's chagrin, was producing a tone better than his.) My sister Deedee turned out to have a magnificent soprano voice, as I have noted elsewhere. David could sing

Family musicians at the piano at Christmastime *(family photo)*

a bit. Though Linda was still a tot, she had a fine voice and would grow up to be part of an a capella group at college.

Once, despite our protests, my father corralled us all around the family piano and had someone take a picture of the would-be von Trapp players for a family Christmas card.

I stuck with the clarinet, and after a while I was good enough to play in the school band. Later, I got together with friends who played the tuba, trumpet, and drums, and we created a small German oompah band on the side.

As my skills improved, I found that I could play extemporaneously. I could improvise and play around as the spirit moved me without any music. When I went off to boarding school, I was emboldened to form a Dixieland band, the Mason-Dixon Five. The Mason-Dixon Five even cut a record with all of us jamming on a loose rendition of "When the Saints Come Marching In."

That was the high point of my clarinet playing. I was pretty good, but I wasn't great. My tone never approached the mellow quality that the finest clarinetists achieve. And I certainly never became a Benny Goodman. It was an early lesson in humility. Whatever you choose to do, there will always be people who can do it better than you. But that's not really the point. For a few years, I was having fun, channeling my inner Benny Goodman, wailing away on my clarinet, enjoying the sheer exuberance of making music.

CHAPTER VII

The World Beyond Irvington

Saturday Was a Workday

In the later part of the 1940s, Saturday was a workday. At least the first half of the day was. Every Saturday morning, my father would get up as usual, have his regular breakfast of a raw egg and tea, walk to the Ardsley-on-Hudson train station, board a train, and travel, courtesy of the Hudson Division of the New York Central Railroad, the twenty-five-mile distance into New York City.

Sometimes he would invite me along. Whether this invitation was intended to be a treat for me or, by getting me out of the house for a while, a treat for my mother was never completely clear. In any event, I regarded it as an adventure and was glad to accompany him into what was for me the mysterious world of the big city.

Irvington was populated by many people whose livelihood depended on jobs in Manhattan. For some of them, Friday was not the end of the workweek. A healthy number would accordingly find themselves on a Saturday morning at the Ardsley station, as Dad did, waiting for the 7:30 train into Grand Central Terminal. Some, like Dad, would then have to catch a subway train all the way down to the bottom of Manhattan. He had to be in the office by 9 o'clock. That was the routine back then for firms in the Financial District. My father's employer, Wood Struthers & Winthrop, was no exception.

After the war, Dad had returned to Wood Struthers. The economy picked up and the firm began to do well. It was small, but in time it became a prominent fixture on Wall Street. It would grow to have a large number of institutional clients and manage several mutual funds. Dad was one of the reasons for this growth. Later, in the 1950s and 1960s, he became widely respected inside and outside of the firm for his cogent analyses of prospective investments, his insightfulness in appraising the quality of company managements, and the rigor of his writing.

My father in his office at Wood Struthers & Winthrop (*family photo*)

He would ultimately rise to become Vice President of Research at Wood Struthers and an officer of Pine Street Mutual Fund. Along the way, on an industry-wide level, he would be instrumental in the creation of the professional designation of Chartered Financial Analyst.

But that was ahead. The events of this short episode took place in the 1940s, while Dad was still earning his spurs at the firm. I was probably seven or eight.

During the summer, the train platform was a sea of straw hats and seersucker suits. Everyone wore a tie. The more stylish of the men—and virtually all of the commuters were men—wore hats with flat crowns and brims called "boaters." When the train arrived, we would board one of the "non-smoking" cars, bypassing the many other cars where smoking was permitted, and settle into our seats. Dad had smoked cigarettes when he was younger but had given up the smoking habit long ago. He was by now virulently anti-smoking. If someone "lit up" in our non-smoker, he would not hesitate to confront the offender and point out that smoking was not allowed in our car.

After a fifty-minute ride, the train would arrive at Grand Central. Here we transferred by shuttle over to the Lexington Avenue Subway and caught a southbound train down to the Wall Street stop, just a short distance from Dad's office. The number of people moving through Grand Central amazed me. Each was seemingly headed toward a different destination and jostling with each other to get there. In a few minutes we successfully negotiated the crowds, arrived at the platform of the Lexington Avenue Subway, and caught a southbound express.

At my insistence, we always made our way to the front car of the subway train. The train operator had his compartment off to one side, but there was always a window in the middle of the very front of the car at which I could stand. There I could see the track ahead and the multi-colored signals that rushed by as we sped along. To make the journey even more exciting, there was a free-spinning wheel located just below the window. It controlled nothing and was essentially useless. Nevertheless, I would always take the wheel in hand and from that commanding position steer the train down to its destination. I must have been pretty good at the job. The train never derailed, and I never failed to get my father to Wall Street.

Since Saturday was a workday, the Wood Struthers office was busy. My father had some real work to do. His challenge was to find a way to keep *me* busy. A yellow pad and a few sharpened pencils would do the trick for an hour or two, but then I would become bored and need some other diversion. A common solution was to put me in the hands of the two ladies who staffed the switchboard. Their job was two-fold: to route calls coming in from outside the office to the right person in the office and to place outgoing calls on behalf of Woods Struthers people who needed to talk with someone outside the office. The switchboard was a large rectangular board with holes and blinking lights. The switchboard operators would sit in front of it, with a small forest of cables and plugs poking up from a stand just in front of them. Each cable represented a different phone line. To connect Mr. Jones from outside the firm with Mr. Milbank inside the firm, an operator would pull up the cable with Mr. Jones's call "on" it and then plug it into the switchboard hole labelled "Mr. Milbank." The operators were quick and adept at making the right connections. You could think of them as the nerve center of the Wood Struthers operation. If the switchboard was busy, there would be numerous cables plugged into numerous holes, often crisscrossing each other as the operators matched multiple callers with multiple recipients. Needless to say, the firm was taking a chance to let me anywhere near such a sensitive function. Nevertheless, the operators seemed to enjoy involving me in their work, occasionally letting me put the plug into what was hopefully the right hole. I must not have fouled up too many sensitive deals. The firm always seemed to remain in business after one of my visits.

After our respective morning duties had been performed, it was time for lunch at Horn & Hardart. This was a highlight of the day. H&H did not serve you at a table. Nor was it an ordinary cafeteria. Instead, it featured something called the "Automat."

The Automat was a wall—several walls, actually—filled with row upon row of little compartments. Each compartment had a glass door so you could see what was in it. Behind the glass door there might be a salad, a chicken

Postcard featuring a Horn & Hardart automat in New York City (*photo by Lumitone Photography, New York; courtesy of Wikimedia Commons*)

pot pie, a piece of fruit, or a slice of cake. You chose what you wanted, put coins into an adjacent slot, twisted a knob and voila! The glass door would swing open, and your food choice was ready for you to take it out. My father always had enough change to get my favorite items: chicken pot pie and lemon meringue pie. For a beverage, we made a sort of lemonade from the water, lemons, and sugar always available at a nearby side station. We would then find a table and chow down. The food was always pretty good, but the main attraction was the neat way you got at it. I never failed to have fun working the Automat.

After lunch, it was time to go home. Back on the subway, I would again commandeer the wheel on the inside of the first car and drive the train, this time back up to midtown. At Grand Central we caught a commuter rail train back up to Irvington, bringing both my father's and my workday to a close.

The Trip to Coney Island That Wasn't

Back when I was growing up, there was a famous amusement park named Coney Island in Brooklyn, New York. It still exists today. It was—and is—well-known for its multiple forms of entertainment, including a roller coaster ride called the Cyclone.

One day, my best friend, Evan Smith, called me to say that his family was going to Coney Island the following week and that they wanted me to come along. Evan's father was a senior vice president of the Pfizer Corporation, one of the world's foremost pharmaceutical manufacturers. This year Pfizer had decided to sponsor a corporate outing at Coney Island. The company was going to take over most of the amusement park for the benefit of its employees, their families, and their guests. Many hundreds of people would be in attendance. As one of Pfizer's most senior officials, Evan's dad had a major role to play. On behalf of the company, he was to be the host. He would be responsible for welcoming everyone and making sure that they had a good time. It was essential that he be there to carry out his duties.

Offers like that didn't come along every day. Coney Island had an almost mythic reputation. I was very excited.

On the appointed day, I got my parents to drive me to the Cedar Ridge section of Irvington where Evan lived. From there, Evan's family, with me in tow, were to drive down to the park and spend the day having a great time.

In my enthusiasm, I had made sure to arrive early. Evan's family would not be leaving for Brooklyn for an hour, so Evan and I decided to kill the time playing in the woods behind his house. These woods were part of a much larger wooded area in that part of Irvington. We had often played there before, rambling across a good portion of the upper part of the village.

It was a beautiful day. This augured well for the Coney Island trip. And it meant that we could enjoy ourselves in the woods in the interim. So, we did. I don't recall specifically what our activities were—probably building a stick fort or climbing the abundant rock outcroppings in the area—but the two of us had a wonderful time. Suddenly feeling hungry and remembering that it would soon be time to leave for Coney Island, we headed back to the house.

Unfortunately, we had been gone for almost three hours, not just one. Evan's father and mother were frantic, first because of their concern for our welfare and then, after our return, because of their upset at our going off on our own and coming back way late. The time had come and gone for the departure to Coney Island. Mr. Smith's role as an official greeter of the company had similarly come and gone. The trip had to be canceled.

For Evan and me, it was the loss of a great time at one of the country's most famous amusement parks. But for Evan's father the consequences were far greater. Because of his stature, his failure to appear at such a major corporate event was a huge embarrassment. He would have to explain the circumstances and apologize to his colleagues.

The relationship between Evan and me and between our families would long outlast that misadventure. For some time afterward, however, he and I were in the doghouse. I was sent home. Evan, I'm afraid, suffered somewhat greater consequences. And we knew, in addition to losing out on a day that could have been fantastic, we had disappointed our parents. It was a lesson, small but keenly felt, in the price of irresponsibility.

Family Vacations

When I was between ten and sixteen, our family vacations usually took place in the out-of-doors. Upstate New York provided many outdoor opportunities. Besides, for parents who would eventually have to foot the bill for four college educations, camping vacations were relatively inexpensive.

Our Chevy station wagon (*family photo*)

Before heading off on a vacation trip, my mother and father would line up all the needed equipment and stow it in the back of our Chevy station wagon. There was a science to this, and they had perfected it. Our gear was packed into the back of the car in layers. It was something like a camping parfait: coolers and other hard items on the floor of the wagon; tents, fishing poles, cooking items, and duffel bags stuffed with clothes in the middle; and sleeping bags and blankets lain over everything to make a level resting place. The highest layer consisted of my sisters, my brother, and me, half-sitting, half-lying on top of it all. Except for what little space we may have been able to carve out, the packing left scant sitting room for us. And not much head room! The several layers filled up virtually all the space behind the front seat. One of us, perhaps my little sister, Linda, when she was a baby, might have been allowed to ride up front. You could do that with the bench seats that cars had in those days. But she would have been the exception. The rest of us wriggled

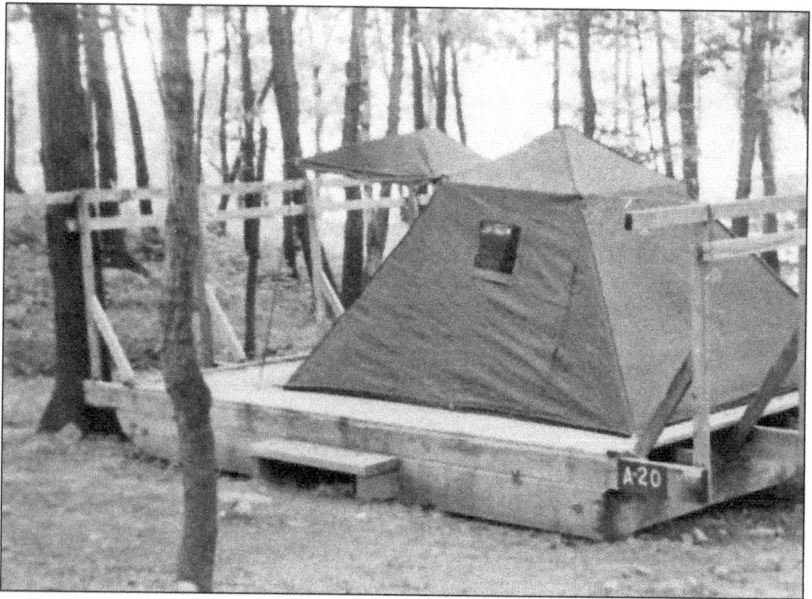

Elegant vacation accommodation (*family photo*)

into the back and rode on top of everything. Car seats had not yet come along. A present-day observer might consider this a precarious situation—and it probably was—but off we went. And we all managed to survive.

The earliest summer vacation trip that I can remember was to a campground near Malone, New York. Malone was a town in the northern part of the state, a couple of hundred miles above Irvington. Getting there meant a long drive in a crowded vehicle. I don't know how my parents managed to keep us in line as we rolled on, mile after lengthy mile.

We made it and had a good time, even with all of us sleeping together in a single tent. The experience created in us a love for camping that continued for many years.

The Catfish

One day my father and I went out on a lake in a rowboat. We were on a fishing expedition. Fishing from a boat was new to me. Up to that point, my history as an angler had been shore-based and modest. I had caught a few sunfish in a pond near our house. I had also caught a couple of small yellow perch while fishing from the banks of the Hudson River. (That was fun, though none of my efforts had ever resulted in anything so spectacular as the long, writhing river eel that my sister Deedee, screaming all the way, had once pulled out of the Hudson.) This time was different. Dad and I were not out there on a lark. Now we were looking for big game. A large-mouth bass, maybe. Or a pickerel.

My fishing tackle was not impressive. It consisted of a simple rod and reel, a handful of hooks, a cup of worms that we had dug up back at the campsite, some ten-pound line, a few lead weights, and a bobber or two. It would have to do. As we rowed out, the lake water was wonderfully clear. We tried different spots. Sometimes I just lowered my rig into them, sometimes I trolled while he rowed. After an hour, I had had only a few nibbles. Possibly they weren't even nibbles. The hook may simply have dragged along the bottom. There were no bass looking to be caught. No pickerel. Not even a sunfish.

As my patience began to run out, Dad maneuvered the boat to still another spot, this one not far from the shore. Here, too, the water was very clear. We drifted a bit, and I could see the bottom moving slowly underneath the boat. And then I saw something else. A catfish. A very big catfish. I could see its whiskers. It seemed unaware that we were just over its head. I was excited. This was my chance. I put a fresh worm on the hook and lowered my line so that the hook, with the new worm on the end, was only a few feet in front of the slowly meandering fish.

Now, any self-respecting bass—or pickerel?—would have taken off at the first sight of the bottom of our boat. Or would have laughed at the jiggling hook and weight and promptly moved along. The catfish did neither of these things. It hardly moved. It made no effort to get away. I raised and lowered the end of my pole to activate the hook and worm combination to attract his attention. There was no response. A minute or two passed. Still no response. The catfish just moseyed along, its whiskers slowly twitching. This was incredibly frustrating. Here was the largest fish I had ever gotten close to, and it was ignoring me.

Finally, throwing caution to the winds, I raised the rod,

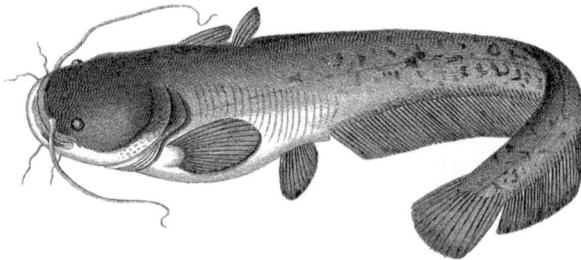

Catfish (*Artwork by Gordon; iStock, with permission*)

which in turn raised the weight near the end of the line, then lowered it quickly so that the weight would hit the fish's back. At last, I got a reaction. Nothing exciting at first. The catfish slowly turned and swam casually over to the nearby worm. It opened its mouth and casually took in the worm and the hook. It was not exactly a strike, such as the ones you might see in videos or fishing publications. But it was a genuine bite. The catfish was on the hook! I could feel the line tighten. Now there was action. The fish began to fight, and the pole bent almost in half. The fish was heavy and determined. I was half standing and half sitting, and the boat was rocking. My arms grew tired. As the fish pulled this way and that, I feared I might lose it.

But I didn't. The hook stayed secure. The line held. After several minutes, adrenalin pumping through my body, I reeled the fish closer. Wow! As it broke the surface of the water, it seemed even bigger than it had down below. My dad had to reach out and grab the line. "It's really a big one!" he said, as he pulled the line with the catfish on it out of the water. Soon the fish was in the boat, flopping at our feet. Dad took the hook out, then passed the catfish over to me. It was wet and slippery and still wriggling. I could barely hold it. I tightened my grip, being careful to avoid its sharp spines. After all that work, I was not about to let my prize go.

To a seasoned sportsman, catching a catfish probably doesn't rate very high. Catfish don't have the silvery appearance or the dashing good looks of a bass. They are bottom feeders and, under the water, they are gray and dull looking. They don't look flashy when they break above the water and fight. But this one had fought and had done so tenaciously. Out of the water, its spines were dangerous. We had no way to weigh it, but it was heavy, far and away the largest fish I had ever caught. Whatever it looked like, catching it was a big deal for me. In my ten-year-old mind, I had at last become a true fisherman.

Sailing at Gilbert Lake State Park

For several years we vacationed at Gilbert Lake State Park in Oneonta, New York. It was our favorite camping venue. The park had log cabins for one- or two-week rentals. They were in high demand. To get one, you had to mail in an application months before, postmarked exactly on a designated day in the late winter. If you were a day early your application would be discarded. If you were a day late, you would either lose out to other applicants or be relegated to a time you didn't want. Fortunately, my parents were careful to get our applications off precisely on time. From the second summer on, they coordinated with another family, the Goffs—whom we got to know on our first trip and who immediately became close friends—so that they and we would always be able to rent cabins at the same time and close to one another.

The cabins were rustic affairs, each with a big stone fireplace, a living room, a small kitchen and eating area, and three bedrooms. My mother and father took one of the bedrooms; we kids slept in bunk beds in the others. There was either a bathroom inside or an outhouse outside. Each cabin was surrounded by woods, with enough room carved out alongside for our car, a picnic table, and a firepit.

The place was delightful during stretches of good weather, but dank and cold when it rained. Typically, when we arrived at our allotted site, we would be moving in on the heels of the family that had just departed. There was always some cleaning up to do. The brunt of this fell on my mother. We each got cleaning assignments but, because she rightly doubted that we had discharged our duties sufficiently, she followed up on each of us. She worked hard the entire first day to make sure that every surface was clean and sanitary. In her zeal to protect us, nothing was left untouched. She always brought a box of aluminum foil on these trips and wrapped foil around the toilet seats—upside and downside—to ensure that no germ would ever touch our tender rear ends.

After claiming our respective sleeping places, we were off and running, first to see whether the Goffs had arrived, then to check out our location. Gilbert Lake was only a short distance away. You could reach it by car or by following a trail through the woods. It didn't take long for us to get into our bathing suits and light out for the beach. A quick run down the trail and you arrived at the park pavilion, with the lake and its beach just beyond. "Last one in is a rotten egg!" we would shout. (We weren't sure what being a rotten egg was like, but, having heard the expression so often, we were certain that it was a state that no one would want to be in.) Soon my sister Deedee, my brother, David, and I were cavorting in the water, splashing one another and our friends and having a grand old time. The beach area was supervised by lifeguards, so my parents generally trusted us to be in the water. We were all good swimmers. David, in fact, was an outstanding swimmer and used to win medals. Linda, the youngest of us, would learn how to swim in time.

Now that we were there, with our summer friends, it felt like our vacation had truly begun.

The lake had more to offer than just swimming. If you qualified, you could rent a rowboat or a canoe by the day or half day at the boat dock. We did this several times.

Rowing was fun, but it was also hard work. The oars were heavy and somewhat beaten up. Furthermore, as you pulled on the oars, you had to keep them in the oarlocks on either side of the boat. On most of the rowboats, the oarlocks were also beaten up. It was apparent that lots of summer vacationers had been out in those boats lots of times over the course of lots of years. The tired condition of the boats, and probably a lack of skill on our part, too, made rowing a challenge. There had to be an easier way.

Aha! We needed a sailboat!

Unfortunately, the park didn't have any sailboats. Undaunted, my friend Bob Goff and I figured that we could make one. Contriving to do this with available materials became an obsession. And, in a manner of speaking, we succeeded in our quest.

To begin with, we needed something that would float. Our only real choices were a rowboat or a canoe. A canoe platform would be lighter and more streamlined but, after rolling over several times, we abandoned that idea. Rowboats were heavy and ungainly, but—no matter—a rowboat would serve as our hull. Next, we needed a mast. We found a tree branch strong and straight enough to serve the purpose. After scrounging up some clothesline, we found a way to lash the branch to one of the rowboat's seats. Lashing a second, smaller branch at right angles near the top of our new "mast," we fashioned a "yard arm." Together, they formed a classic "square rig." For a sail, we pressed a large poncho into service and tied more clothesline to its lower corners. We were ready. Let the wind do the work!

The prevailing breezes ran from the boat area all the way down to the foot of the lake, roughly half a mile away. We maneuvered our craft into position. It was ungainly and top-heavy, but if we sat on either side of the boat, it stayed upright. The poncho filled with the breeze. We were under way!

Because our rigging was so crude, the only direction we could go was straight down wind, but this we did very well. We kept the poncho full of wind. Our pace picked up. The next minutes were glorious. We were ecstatic—running before the wind, our "spinnaker" billowing out ahead. Our feelings were triumphal. There we were, sailing on the bounding main!

Well, maybe not quite. It was more like slowly gliding on the placid surface of the lake. Still, in fifteen to twenty minutes, we reached the foot of the lake. We landed our erstwhile sailboat and tied it up to a nearby rock. Mission accomplished! It was only then that we realized the predicament we had created for ourselves. How were we going to get back to the boat dock, which was now half a mile in the other direction? And upwind, besides. Our "sailboat" couldn't go against the wind. We wouldn't be able to tack our way back! The unhappy reality of our situation was now apparent. We would have to dismantle our beautiful creation, knot by knot, and branch by branch. And, with the wind now in our faces, row our way back.

Capturing the Wild Red Eft

The red eft is a small salamander. Not yet fully mature, it is only three or four inches long. It's a light shade of orange with red spots on its back. The woods around our cabin in Gilbert Lake State Park were full of red efts, crawling over the moss and hiding under the rocks and rotting logs that lay all about. They were irresistible. Deedee, David, and I—probably Linda, too, when she was older—spent hours searching for them, catching them in our hands, and playing with them.

As fascinated as we were by the efts, they were no doubt less than fascinated by us children as we ran after them,

Red eft in its wooded habitat (*photo by James Robert Smith; iStock, with permission*)

tearing up their habitat and terrifying them with our exuberance. Channeling our inner naturalist, we spent hours fashioning terraria in which to house them. These would-be homes began with cardboard boxes. We would fill a box with an inch or two of dirt, lay a sheet of moss on top of the dirt, add a few rocks with spaces between for the efts to hide in, and finish the terrarium off with sticks from the vicinity in which the hapless animals had been caught. Add a little water and—voila!—you had a comfortable eft dwelling. Or so, in our naivete, we thought. Yet we did all this with a degree of scientific interest, even benevolence. How would they fare? What could we do to improve their surroundings? Did they need more rocks? Should we add water? First thing in the morning and last thing at night we checked on them. If one had died, we sadly laid it to rest back in the woods and added another to the box. It was important, we thought, that each eft should have company.

The efts survived for a while, but despite our best efforts—or perhaps because of them—their mortality rate was high.

At the end of one summer, we decided to bring one of the cardboard-box terraria back home with us, together with its inhabitants. The box was precariously stowed in a corner in the back of the station wagon, amidst all the gear. Happily, it and the efts inside survived the journey.

Home once again, we took the box behind our house. A day or so later, after admiring the efts one last time, we released them. It must have been a tough transition. Creatures that had been accustomed to a shady wood in Oneonta, New York, suddenly found themselves in the ecosystem of an Irvington, New York, backyard. Our small charges crawled off in search of something familiar: some moss maybe, a rotting log, some rocks to hide under, a little moisture. Looking back, I expect that they were disappointed. Conditions here were inexorably different from the moist and wooded environment they had known. Subjecting them to this new environment amounted to giving them a death sentence. As good as our intentions were, most of the efts probably died within a week.

In our childish way, we were sad to think of this. But our sadness produced at least some good. It awakened in us deeper empathy for our fellow creatures. It taught us that we were not really capable of making a proper home for them outside their native habitat. And, perhaps, it even led to an embryonic understanding that environments are critical for all of us and not something that one should meddle with.

Arrowheads from the Stone Age

When I was ten, a bump appeared on the upper part of my right arm. It was diagnosed as an osteochondroma, which is a benign bone tumor. Though it was not cancerous, my parents decided that I should have it removed. They took me to the Sloan Kettering Institute, a hospital in New York City. Sloan Kettering is famous for its expertise in dealing with cancer. A surgeon removed the growth, and after the operation, I spent the next four days in the hospital recuperating.

When I woke up after the procedure, I found that I had a roommate. He was an older man who suffered from the real thing, cancer of the lung. He had had a whole lung removed. I could tell that his case was serious by the number of stitches that he had. My incision took only seven or eight stitches. He had what seemed like dozens. We were usually separated by a curtain, but when his nurse changed his dressing, I got a glimpse of them. They went down his chest, all the way around his waist, and up again on his back.

My roommate was undoubtedly in some pain, but he was cheerful and friendly to talk with. It turned out that he was an executive of the Arabian American Oil Company, also known as Aramco. Though he was an American, he had spent the better part of his adult life in Saudi Arabia, prospecting for oil and managing some of the company's drilling activities. In the four days we were together, he took a shine to his young roommate—me—and we had several interesting conversations.

One day, he asked me whether I was interested in arrowheads. Well, of course I was! I was thoroughly imbued with a fascination for cowboys and Indians, the Lone Ranger, Tom Mix, and anything else having to do with the Wild West. When I showed my interest, he went on to ask whether I wanted some. This was too good to be true. Sure, I said. He responded by saying that he might have some and would think about it.

Two days later, he had a visitor. It was his wife. She had a small jar with her and in it were two dozen pieces of chipped stone. I want you to have these arrowheads, he said. She brought the jar over to my bed. I could hardly contain my excitement. I reached into the jar to touch them. There they were, real arrowheads, undoubtedly shot by real American Indians. How old are they? I asked, expecting to hear a really big number. A number like one hundred or maybe two hundred, even.

They're about five thousand years old, he said. They date back to the Stone Age and were made by the ancient people who lived in Saudi Arabia at the time. I found them over the years I was working there, he continued, walking around the desert.

It was more than I could comprehend. Arrowheads made by Arabians? Thousands of years ago? All of that was beyond anything I had ever imagined, but he gently explained that primitive peoples in many parts of the world had fashioned weapons and tools like these long before Wyatt Earp ever came along. It finally got through to me. These arrowheads were very old, indeed. A lot more than a few hundred years. I had been given a rare treasure.

Over the years, I have kept the arrowheads in a jar of my own. A cleaned-out peanut-butter jar. I still have most of them. I keep them in our safe at home, awaiting the day when one or more grandchildren might prize them as much as I do and be fitting recipients.

But I haven't saved all of them for that purpose. Seven or eight years ago, I had an opportunity to host a luncheon in honor of Turki al Faisal, a member of the Saudi royal family and then the Arabian ambassador to the United States. Imagining what a worthy token of his visit might be, I hit upon the notion of making him a gift of five of the arrowheads. A friend in the business of fine picture framing took on the challenge of doing something special with them for presentation purposes. After giving the matter thought, he designed and crafted a beautiful, velvet-lined shadow box and arrayed the arrowheads in it. With the finest of threads, he stitched them into place. The display was beautiful.

Arabian arrowhead display presented to Saudi ambassador
(*family photo*)

On the day of the luncheon, I told the story of how I came to have the arrowheads and presented the shadow box to the ambassador. These five ancient stones have had an adventure, I said. Now they are ready to return home. It was quite a surprise for the ambassador, and its effect on him was wonderful to see. Accepting the gift, he spoke effusively about how meaningful it was. At the end of the affair, he added that he would see to it that the five arrowheads, together with the exquisite box in which they were housed, would be put on display in the royal museum in Riyadh.

Saudi Arabia is a controversial country. In addition to relegating women to second-class status, it has taken a variety of other actions in recent years that have earned it international condemnation. For geopolitical reasons and the sake of its oil reserves, it nevertheless remains an American ally. I have never been there, and at this point doubt that I will ever go. But I would love to know whether the ambassador followed through. Did the five arrowheads and their beautiful box make it to the royal museum? If you ever go there, would you take a look?

Searching for the "Inverted Jenny"

I must have inherited a collecting gene from my father. He was a coin collector. He collected coins of all kinds. Later in his life, he specialized in "proof" coins, unblemished coins that had never been in circulation after being minted.

When I began collecting, I went in a different direction, collecting postage stamps. Almost every country has a mail service and publishes stamps in different denominations, sizes, and colors. Many of them are beautiful. Once a stamp has been used on a letter and canceled by the post office, its value decreases. Unless the stamp has become old and rare, that is. Then it might have a high value. The rarer the better! Canceled or not, stamps make great collectibles. I loved their variety and set about to have as many different kinds as I could. I bought stamp-collecting books that had black-and-white images of all the stamps that a given country had published, arranged by date of issue. I would then try to find stamps to match the images, sometimes by going to stamp-collecting conventions, sometimes by raiding boxes of old correspondence that I found in my family's attic, sometimes by trading stamps with another collector.

And sometimes I bought large bags of unsorted stamps gathered by merchants in the stamp collection business expressly for people like me to sort through. I loved sorting through the bags; it was like a treasure hunt. When I found a stamp that I hadn't seen before, I would add it to my collection. To do this, I folded a small piece of sticky cellophane called a "hinge," attached it on the back of the stamp, found the right country and the right page in my collecting book, and placed the stamp and hinge combination on top of the appropriate image. As a page began to fill up, I would take pride in having collected so many of the called-for stamps. Seeing all of them on the same page, similar in some respects but each of them different in one way or another, was interesting to me. I was, I guess, developing a primitive ability to compare like things while observing the contrasts between them.

Every now and then, I discovered an unusual stamp, one that was hard to find. It could be valuable if the stamp was very old and no longer in circulation, or if not very many of its variety had been printed in the first place, or if a mistake had been made on the first batch printed that was subsequently corrected in later batches, creating a small pool of stamps never to be printed that way again. These were rare collectors' items, sometimes worth a lot of money.

The stamp I most wanted to find was the "Inverted Jenny." Back in 1918, the U.S. Post Office issued a twenty-four-cent stamp. In its middle, the stamp featured an image of a biplane that was commonly used to carry mail in the early days of airmail. The biplane was a model called the "Jenny." Millions of the stamps were printed and printed correctly. With a batch of one hundred stamps, though, the printer slipped up. Instead of printing the plane right side up, it printed the plane upside down.

That error made the misprinted stamps, the Inverted Jennys, very rare and valuable. They were fetching tens of thousands of dollars each. (Much later, in 2021, a single Inverted Jenny would be said to be worth $1,350,000!) I was always on the alert, hoping that an Inverted Jenny would show up in one of those large bags of unsorted stamps, having slipped through unnoticed when the bag was being filled!

The Inverted Jenny never flew into my arms, but lots of beautiful and interesting stamps did. Some were quite valuable in a monetary sense. Most, of course, were just average. But each new and different stamp was important to me. I was intrigued to see what it told about its country and about who and what was regarded as important there. Moreover, gathered together in the pages of my collecting book, the stamps told an even larger story: the great story of the

The much sought-after "Inverted Jenny" postage stamp (*iStock, with permission*)

way in which the world's postal services have connected human beings together, enabling commerce and civilization to flourish. Building my collection and watching that story unfold in the process gave me great satisfaction.

SUBSEQUENTLY, I moved beyond stamp collecting. I collected baseball cards, rocks with unusual mineral properties, and topographic maps—all manner of things. Later, as an adult, I built a large collection of truly rare and valuable antique maps from the sixteenth, seventeenth, and eighteenth centuries, most of which I have donated to Villanova University. They now form the university's John F. and Susan B. Smith Map Collection.

My collecting activities have been varied, but they have had this virtue in common: They taught me to see the similarities among like things and the differences between them. This lesson has proven helpful throughout my life, even in the pursuit of my career as a trial lawyer. A litigation attorney who is good at finding supportive precedents and distinguishing those that are adverse is likely to prevail on behalf of his or her client.

CHAPTER VIII

Lessons

I Try Smoking

I will be forever grateful for my first—and disastrous—attempts to smoke.

The dead limbs of one of the trees in our backyard used to drop twigs that were porous and light. I found that I could suck on the ones that had dried out and draw air through them. Because I could push air into and pull air out of them, I called them "puffer sticks."

Smoking was a common habit of adults in the 1940s and 1950s. It was glorified in the movies of the era. Naturally I tried to imitate it. I would break off a four-inch length of puffer stick, stick it in my mouth, and walk around as if I were the coolest kid in the world. But real cigarette smokers light their cigarettes. So, what I was doing with an unlit puffer stick wasn't really cool. I had to try the real thing.

It wasn't long before I found a corner of the yard where I wouldn't be seen and tried to light one of the puffer sticks. This turned out to be difficult. It pretty much required that I hold a lighted match continuously to the end I wanted to light. Well, if that's what it took, I would do it. I would light match after match until I got the thing going. Sometimes this worked and I could get the end to smolder. Now here was something that I could really smoke. I put the other end back in my mouth and drew in a breath. Not much came through. I tried again. This time my effort was rewarded. A big puff of acrid smoke came into my mouth and lungs. Unfortunately, it immediately set off a fit of coughing. My eyes were burning. The smoke stunk. I couldn't get it out of my mouth or nose. I was suddenly sick to my stomach. It took a while before I dared go back into the house. When I went back in, I blew my nose and washed my face and hands. I don't think I fooled my mother, but she didn't say anything.

The next day, I sneaked away again. I'm not sure what I was expecting. In any event, safely out of sight, I "lit up" another puffer "cigarette." I was hoping for a better result, but it was not to be. I coughed again. My eyes burned again. I got sick to my stomach again. This was decidedly *not* cool. I had had enough. My experiment with puffer sticks came to an end.

Later in my life, I tried smoking real cigarettes. Later still, I tried a pipe. Cigarette tobacco was not as putrid as my puffer sticks had been. I actually liked the smell of pipe tobacco. Still, whatever I tried to smoke, it ended up disagreeing with me. One way or another, smoking made me sick. I finally took my early puffer stick lesson to heart. Smoking and I were not made for each other.

Sports Medicine: "Just Rub It Off"

I liked sports as a youngster. All kinds of sports. They helped me to grow. And grow up. Through sports, I learned new skills. I learned what I might be good at and what I probably wouldn't be good at. I learned about teamwork. And I learned the importance of developing toughness.

The game of baseball taught me some of this.

Irvington had a little league of sorts. It was informal and probably not officially sanctioned. It just served our town. One of the baseball teams in the league was called the Red Devils. That was my team.

It's 1953. I'm twelve years old. The Red Devils are playing a game in Irvington's Memorial Park against another team in the town league. I'm the first baseman. My best friend, Evan Smith, is on the team, too. The Red Devils are pretty good. At least, we hustle. Our coach, Phil, is big on hustling. Around the third or fourth inning, I'm up at bat . . .

I'm not sure exactly why I became a first baseman, but it had something to do with my throwing the ball left-handed. We lefties have an advantage playing first base. For some odd reason, though, I batted right-handed. I wasn't a power hitter, but I could stand up to the plate, see the ball, and make a fair number of singles and doubles. Of course, in a league with pitchers who were young and lacked control, you could also get hit by a wild pitch.

. . . so, there I am, waiting for the next pitch. One of my Red Devil teammates is on first base. I'm planning to lay down a bunt to advance him from first to second. The count is one and one. I step closer to the plate, crowding it in preparation for the bunt. The pitcher throws. It's a fast ball. Too late I realize that it's coming in way inside. As I turn away, it hits me in the ribs and sends me sprawling. The wind has been knocked out of me. I am stunned for a moment. Then sensation comes back. My ribs are stinging. Wow, does it hurt! For a few minutes, play stops. Phil comes over. I'm thinking that I am through for the day. Someone will come in from the bench and replace me. As a struck batter, I am entitled to go to first base automatically, but another Red Devil will take my place.

Phil leans down to assess my injury. I don't see how I can continue in the game. I'm ready to leave the field. However, he will have none of it. He stands me up, lifts my shirt, and takes a close look at the bruise. It's purple and red. "Must have hurt," he says. Then he looks me in the eye and dispenses a classic piece of sports medical advice: "Just rub it off, son. Just rub it off!" With that, he directs me toward first base. I'm a bit dazed and still nursing my ribs. But I dutifully trot down the line. Pain or no pain, I am now a base runner. "Play ball!" Phil shouts, and the game goes on.

In the course of my life, I have suffered injuries significantly more painful than being hit by a baseball. They weren't always physical. A few involved losing something: a game, a case, a relationship. As someone who is very competitive and likes to win, injuries like those were particularly painful. But, whatever the injury, I have come to realize that the important question is always: How do you respond to it? In the homely example of my injury on the baseball field, my coach was saying, don't dwell on it. If need be, learn from your injury and then carry on. His words still echo in my mind. Nurse your hurt for a few moments but get past it. It's time once again to play ball.

The Day I Shot a Squirrel

My father was an owner of firearms. And a great respecter of them. He owned two guns. One was a .22-caliber rifle that was used mostly as a shotgun for trap shooting at clay pigeons. The other was a .45-caliber pistol like the one that he carried when he was in the Army during World War II.

The .22 was kept in the deep recesses of a closet in Dad and Mom's bedroom, hidden behind the hanging clothes. The .45 was kept at a safer distance. It was in a wooden box up in our attic.

Dad would bring the .22 out for trap-shooting parties that he would conduct from our backyard.

Our house was built high up on a long hillside overlooking the Hudson River. Running along the river were the tracks of the Hudson Division of the New York Central Railroad. They must have been about a quarter mile below our fence line. In the 1940s, before any houses were built below us, there was nothing between us and the railroad tracks, only an empty meadow and trees. We may not have been in the country, but we certainly weren't in the suburbs, either.

Dad had boxes of clay pigeons and a heavy, spring-loaded launcher in the basement. On an appointed occasion, he would bring a box of clay pigeons up, position the launcher in the backyard facing down the hill, and invite our neighbors to try their hands. Everyone got to shoot in turn, with Dad presiding. The first time I remember being invited to shoot, Dad gave me a lecture on gun safety. And he made me clean the rifle after it was all over.

I confess to having been fascinated. This was not horseplay with cap guns. This was the real thing. I enjoyed it.

My father was also involved in the affairs of our village, first as a director of the Irvington Community Association and, years later, as an elected trustee of the village. In that later capacity, he would, among other things, assume an administrative role as Irvington's police commissioner. Well before that time, though, he enjoyed a close relationship with the village police, who respected his wartime service.

The Irvington police force was small, like the village itself, but it underwent training just like its counterparts in larger municipalities. Among other things, this meant that the members of the force had to maintain their proficiency in the use of firearms, particularly in the use of .45 pistols. They regularly trained at a local shooting range, which had both an indoor and an outdoor facility. Even before he was elected as a trustee and took on the duties of a commissioner, Dad often shot with them. Now and then he brought me along.

To this day, I remember the noise of multiple .45s going off, particularly in the indoor portion of the range. As I watched the men shoot, my father among them, I was stunned by the sound. The initial reports of the firing weapons and their reverberations off the hard cement side walls were deafening.

On a later occasion, amidst all the men who were practicing, I was given a try. I took hold of the gun. Mindful of my instruction, I kept it pointing downward and facing forward toward the wall where the targets were posted. It was heavy in my grip. Even using two hands, a .45 pistol is hard to hold. At least for a kid. I was nervous. Determined not to embarrass my father, I stepped up to the line, took aim as best I could, and fired. Bang! The kick of the weapon was ferocious. The instruction session had not prepared me for the recoil. My wrists hurt long after the echoes had died down.

But I had done it. Though I was only shooting at a paper target posted on a wall and probably missed it altogether on that first attempt, I had done it. In some primal sense, I had become, I suppose, the juvenile equivalent of a "true" man.

Over the next couple of years, I went several more times to the police range with my father. I never became truly accustomed to the noise or the recoil, but I held my own. I also participated in the trap-shooting activities whenever they occurred in the backyard.

Going to summer camp in the 1950s gave me more opportunities to learn about guns. Camp Sloane was a YMCA camp near the northwest corner of Connecticut. The National Rifle Association (NRA) sponsored junior marksman sessions there. The NRA was a different organization then. The organization was about marksmanship, hunting game, and gun safety. The modern reputation of the organization as a group that will fight even sensible gun control measures hadn't taken hold.

At Camp Sloane, we shot .22 rifles, like the rifle that Dad owned, using a small range off to the side of the camp property. The camp counselor in charge took safety very seriously. As we learned about the weapons and how to shoot them, we would first receive a small metal achievement pin and then, as we progressed in our skill levels, we would receive a succession of bars to hang off the pin. I reached the level of Senior Marksman.

Although gun safety and respect for firearms had been drilled into me, I had also become intrigued with guns and comfortable around them, probably too much so. One summer, reading a comic book, I saw an ad for Daisy Air Rifles. As the name suggests, the Daisy Air Rifle was air-powered. A long lever ran from the middle of the gun down along and underneath the stock. You would pull the lever down as far as it would go and then push it back into place. This would charge a compartment in the barrel with compressed air. It would also lodge a small metal pellet into the barrel. The action was a little bit like that of a shotgun.

The air rifle was sold as a toy for older kids. It lacked the explosive force of a real rifle and was advertised as not being particularly dangerous. The metal pellets were the size of small beads, not bullets. How dangerous could it be if you could order one out of a comic book? I had to have one. I somehow managed to get my parents to give me permission. For target practice, I told them. And yes, I would be careful.

Of course, over the years, many a child or pet has been hurt by these so-called toys. Painful welts raised. Eyes permanently blinded.

When the shiny new Daisy arrived, I was beside myself with excitement. It worked like a charm. The chamber for pellets could hold quite a number at one time. The pumping action would compress the air and put the pellet into place, and it was ready to fire. It was easy. To reload, you just pumped, and it was ready to fire again. Virtually like a semi-automatic weapon. I would go into the backyard, set some tin cans or bottles on a log, and plunk away. Or go into the woods behind our house and shoot at trees. Sometimes alone and sometimes with friends. Often, I was just plain reckless. I never pointed the air rifle at anyone, but I played at war games with it, running toward some objective, hitting the dirt, rolling, and firing. Playing with the Daisy was a daily activity, mostly during weekdays after school. My dad was away at work. My mom was usually home but was not aware—I thought—of what I was doing. I was careful not to display my prowess as a charging infantryman in her presence.

However reckless I had become, I never actually injured anyone. But something worse had happened. I had become blasé with a firearm.

Surrounded by woods and fields, our house often had animal visitors. Sometimes they came to stay. A rat snake lived under a sawn-off stump in the northern part of the yard. We could walk quietly up to the stump, lift it up on its side, and see him neatly coiled up in the depression below the stump. We called him the "Lone Ranger." He had a placid personality, and because he didn't harm us, we children regarded him almost as a pet. We'd replace the stump and let him be. On the west side of the house, wisteria climbed up to the second floor. It was the home of a variety of wildlife, of which the most interesting were the praying mantises. They were probably a terror to other insect species, and the female of the species was reputed to eat the males, but from our vantage point they were simply a slow-moving, gigantic, somewhat exotic bug. As in the case of our friend the Lone Ranger, there was no reason for us to take offense at their presence. And when a rabbit occasionally appeared in the yard, we were positively joyful.

Ah, but the squirrels. Red squirrels. Indiscrete creatures. Rather than living in the many trees that were available around the yard, they chose to live in the attic. There they took advantage of our unwitting hospitality, gnawing on whatever suited their fancy, endangering electrical circuits by chewing on the insulation, making noise overhead, and leaving little calling cards of excrement about the attic floor. The trees that stood near the house and the branches that hung over the roof would have made dandy abodes. Instead, our live-in squirrel neighbors regarded the tree trunks and limbs merely as highways in and out of the attic.

Dad was one of the most even-tempered men on the planet, but the squirrels brought out a side to him that most people never saw. He disliked them intensely. He tried plugging holes, cutting off any potential entrances. He tried traps. He strewed moth balls about the attic to make their lives unpleasant. Nothing worked.

I observed all of this and felt his frustration. What could be done, I said to myself, that had not already been tried? Then after weeks of uncertainty, the solution came to me in a flash of inspiration. I would shoot the little intruders.

Now I was an obedient son. I generally hewed to the straight-and-narrow path. Rare were the instances where I directly violated what I knew my parents would want or not want done, implicitly or otherwise. The .22 was off limits.

Untouchable. I knew that. But I also knew that the Daisy Air Rifle would not get the job done. This mission required real firepower. Yes, a real rifle, not an air rifle. It required the .22.

One afternoon, I acted. After coming home from school, I entered my parents' bedroom, opened the closet door, found the rifle and a box of ammunition, and withdrew, gun in hand, as quickly as I had entered. My heart was pounding. This activity was not authorized. Still, I said to myself, I had a job to do. It was not for me but for my family. I was helping my dad. Besides, having been several times to a genuine police firing range and, moreover, possessing the credential—drum roll, please—of Senior Marksman, I knew what I was doing!

My mother was aware of what was going on even before I got outside the house. She saw the .22, and asked me in a gentle voice what I planned to do with it. I told her what I intended to do. Are you sure? she said. Full of self-importance, the sheer nobility of my undertaking, and the impetuosity of youth, I said I was.

Biding her time, she allowed my small drama to unfold.

I loaded the rifle. The ammunition that I had taken was the same ammunition that was used in the trap-shooting parties. Shells with shot in them, not bullets. It would have to do. I took up a position twenty-five feet or so from one of the trees that was so often used by the squirrels to get into the house and sat down to wait.

It didn't take long for a squirrel to appear. He was climbing on a tree. Suddenly, there he was, staring at me. A perfect target. I couldn't miss. I took aim and fired.

Sometimes events unfold precisely as one expects. Sometimes they don't. And sometimes they spin off unexpectedly, leaving you unsure of what has just happened and what will happen next.

The pieces of shot reached their target square on. They tore into the little animal's chest and legs. For what seemed

Suddenly, there he was . . . (*photo by Dynamite 16 – Own Work; courtesy of Wikimedia Commons*)

like minutes but were really seconds, he desperately tried to maintain his hold on the tree. Then, bleeding, he fell to the ground.

It had been a perfect shot, but it brought about a most terrible, imperfect result. What lay before me was not a pest well rid of. It was a creature in agony. He writhed in pain for a long time, his paws scratching the air. His movements gradually slowed. As I watched, a wave of agony broke over me. I had not killed a squirrel; I had destroyed a life. I felt dizzy. As he breathed his last breaths, jerking spasmodically at my feet, tears flooded my eyes. I was overwhelmed by remorse.

"Johnny," my mother called out the back door, "it's time to come in."

I came back into the house. Mom disapproved of what I had done, but she knew that my self-reproach was great and that she didn't need to add her own. She was wise in that way. She was allowing me to learn, and in that way making me learn, the lesson I was in the process of teaching myself.

After a time, she asked what I was going to do with the dead squirrel. "I will bury him in the backyard," I said. "That seems like the right thing to do," she replied. I dug a pit, laid him in it, and covered the hole with dirt.

By the time my father returned home from work, it was

all over. I had cleaned the gun and put it back in the closet. Mom told him about the incident, of course. I don't remember everything he said to me later. He must have told me that I had done a foolish and dangerous thing and that he was disappointed by my actions. Beyond that, however, he, too, seemed content to let me wrestle on my own with what I had done. Which I most definitely did for a long time afterward.

Epilogue

After the tenth grade, I went away to boarding school. That experience would be followed in due course by college, four years in the Navy, and law school. I would marry an extraordinary and beautiful person. We moved to Philadelphia and raised three remarkable children. I had a challenging but satisfying legal career and many opportunities to perform public service.

Much of the person I was to become, though, was formed when I was just a kid. As the stories in this book reflect, I had ups that filled me with joy, downs that sobered me, and funny experiences that helped me grow a sense of humor. Good or bad, they all had a hand in shaping me. An author by the name of Robert Fulghum once wrote a book entitled *All I Really Need to Know I Learned in Kindergarten*. The experiences of my boyhood performed much the same service for me.

I've discovered that the business of going through highs and lows doesn't stop just because you become an adult. Nevertheless, my childhood helped prepare me for what lay ahead. I learned a lot. I began to understand things. I became more resilient. Growing up, I grew up.

All things considered, I have had a wonderful life.

I hope the same for you.

Acknowledgments

No project of this scope can be accomplished without the help of others. I received assistance from many quarters, and it is a pleasure to acknowledge them here.

My siblings, Mary Dake Smith Ryerson, David Maulsby Smith, and Linda Mairs Smith-Shearer participated in or witnessed more than a few of the events described in the memoir, as did my oldest boyhood friend, Evan Smith. I drew upon their recollections to check my own. My brother, David, was kind enough to provide me with the image of a painting that graces his living room of our great-great-grandfather, Col. William P. Maulsby. It is reproduced here. Other family members, now deceased, left behind correspondence, notes, and photographs that were of great help in piecing together their histories. The quality of the older photographs leaves something to be desired, but they are what I have, and I have used them liberally throughout. Beyond the photographs, a set of genealogical records assembled by my maternal grandmother, Mary Dake Mattison Mairs, and a file of my father's U.S. Army records were of considerable usefulness. Finally, my son Stephen True Smith, while obviously not a participant in my boyhood adventures, was nevertheless able to make a variety of suggestions for improving the manuscript.

When I was unable to unearth just the right picture to illustrate one or more of the stories, several image services came to my rescue and provided me with generic or thematically related pictures that were close enough that I felt comfortable using them. The services have been credited accordingly. I would, though, like to take special note of two pictures by individual photographers. One, by Edna Kornberg, is a view shot in black-and-white that looks up toward Main Street from the Hudson River. Her use of a telephoto lens exaggerates the steepness of the street. But not by much! Main Street's steady rise from the river is one of its chief and most endearing characteristics. The second, taken by the late Jake Rajs, is a more modern view looking down the other way on Main Street, this time toward the river. It is a beautiful and colorful picture and is a tribute to Rajs's professional skill. His daughter, Chloe, graciously made it available from the Jake Rajs Archive. I could not help but to put it on the back cover of the book. In both of these cases, the donors provided the photographs gratis.

I wish also to take note of the Irvington Historical Society and its President, Veronica Gedrich. Ms. Gedrich was extremely helpful in providing leads to photographs and other information about the Village of Irvington. She was also kind enough to review the manuscript before publication.

That leaves the two persons without whom the memoir would simply not have been possible.

One of these persons is my editor, Deborah S. Smith. Debby is gifted, skilled, and patient. Though I have fancied myself as a good writer, going all the way back to seventh grade and the rigor of Mrs. Bishop's English class, I frequently needed Debby's help while I was writing. Her diplomatically put suggestions for improvement were often right on the mark. In sum, she made significant contributions to the several chapters and then, as it started to come together, to the memoir as a whole. She even introduced me to my excellent book designer, Douglas Gordon, and his firm, New Door Books. For each and all of these things, I am grateful.

Finally, and most important, I need to thank the extraordinary person that I met in 1965 and married two years later. Susan Brown Smith has been my life companion of fifty-seven years. Throughout that period, she has been a counselor, supporter, constructive critic, and cheerleader. Over the past six months in particular, she allowed me the time and space to focus on telling the stories in this memoir. Of course, her contributions go much deeper than that. If I have had a wonderful life, as I claim in the Epilogue, her love and caring are the principal reasons. They have buoyed me in everything I have done.

Villanova, Pennsylvania
April 2022

.

www.ingramcontent.com/pod-product-compliance
Ingram Content Group UK Ltd.
Pitfield, Milton Keynes, MK11 3LW, UK
UKHW040926281224
3814UKWH00001B/73